NOVEMBER

Make the Most of Every Month with Carson-Dellosa's Monthly Books!

Production Manager
Chris McIntyre

Editorial Director
Jennifer Weaver-Spencer

Writers
Lynette Pyne
Amy Gamble
Julie Eick Granchelli

Editors
Carol Layton
Kelly Gunzenhauser
Maria McKinney
Tracy Soles

Art Directors
Penny Casto
Alain Barsony

Art Coordinator
Edward Fields

Illustrators
Mike Duggins
Erik Huffine
David Lackey
Ray Lambert
George Ling
Bill Neville
Betsy Peninger
J.J. Rudisill
Pam Thayer
Todd Tyson
Julie Webb

Cover Design
Amber Kocher Crouch
Ray Lambert
J.J. Rudisill

Carson-Dellosa Publishing Company, Inc.

NOVEMBER

Table of Contents

NOVEMBER TEACHER TIPS

Welcome New Students

Make the transition easier for new students who enter your class after the school year has started. Appoint one student to act as a tour guide to show the student where classroom supplies are located and give a tour of the school. Choose another student to act as a lunch buddy to sit with the new student. Assign a recess buddy or buddies to play with the new student on the playground. This will help your newest class member meet several people from the start.

Comment Folders

Keep the lines of communication between you and parents open using homework comment folders. Give each child a folder with a sheet of paper stapled to the outside with spaces for the date, comments, and parent initials. Students should take the homework folders home and parents should comment and initial the sheet when assignments are returned. Refer to the comment sheets during parent conferences for a quick review of student progress.

Reusable Graphs

On poster board, draw blank graphs to be used throughout the year. Laminate each graph. Use overhead markers to program each graph, then erase and reuse them.

Fun Classroom Parties

When planning a classroom party, include several small group activities, such as cooking, crafts, and games. Set up each activity at a different table and have a parent volunteer help at each area. Divide students into small groups and allow the groups to rotate around the room to each area.

Save Your Charts

Keep classroom charts and posters free from wear and tear. Staple clear acetate to a bulletin board, leaving the top open. Add a decorative touch by stapling colored border strips around the three closed edges. Slide charts or posters into this protective pocket and change the displays as desired.

Seasonal Worksheets

Copy seasonal puzzle, game, or activity pages and mount them on poster board. Cut out and laminate the worksheets and place them in a folder with an overhead marker. When a child has free time, let him complete a worksheet. When finished, students can erase the pages and place them back in the folder.

November

Day-by-Day Calendar

1 *National Author's Day* Have children design book jackets for their favorite books.

2 *Daniel Boone's Birthday* Born in 1734, he traveled and lived in many places in the United States. Have children illustrate and write about a place they would like to live.

3 The *first animal, a Russian dog named Laika, was sent into space* on this day in 1957. Ask each student to discuss how he would feel if his family pet were sent into space. What would he miss most about the animal? What would the animal miss most about him?

4 *National Children's Goal-Setting Day* Make a *We're Reaching for the Stars!* bulletin board with the class. On construction paper stars, have students write small goals they would like to achieve. Post the stars on the bulletin board.

5 *Susan B. Anthony fined for voting* Have the boys in the class vote for a free-time activity and then allow the girls to vote on another issue. Ask students how they felt when they were not allowed a vote.

6 *James Naismith's Birthday* The inventor of basketball was born in 1861. Let students take turns tossing a soft foam ball into a basket from several distances. Measure the distances.

7 *Archaeologist Howard Carter found the entrance to Pharaoh Tutankhamen's tomb* on this day in 1922. Take some time today to teach the class about this young king. Ask students to write or tell if they would want to be king at such a young age.

8 *Milton Bradley's Birthday* The game maker was born in 1836. Have students work with partners to create a game.

9 *Benjamin Banneker's Birthday* The African-American astronomer was born in 1731. Using black paper and chalk, have children draw constellations and name them.

10 *Sesame Street's Debut* The television show, featuring puppets, first aired in 1969. Have students bring in socks and create puppets by gluing yarn and fabric scraps to them.

11 *International Creative Child Month* Give students a free period to do something creative. At the end of the period, have them share with the class what they have done.

12 The *Space Shuttle Columbia first flew* on this day in 1981. Have students write a journal about a space shuttle flight. What would it feel like? What would they see?

13 *The World Scrabble® Championship* is held on this day. Hold a class Scrabble® Championship or use a Scrabble® dictionary to teach the class a new word.

14 *Children's Day in India* is celebrated today. Have students create and decorate banners for the occasion.

4

5 **American Education Week** Have students tell or write about their favorite school subjects this week.

6 **Chocolate chips went on sale for the first time** on this day in 1939. Make chocolate chip cookies with the class.

17 **Peanut Butter Lover's Month** Let students sample creamy and crunchy peanut butter. Then, have them list adjectives describing the texture and taste of each kind.

8 **Mickey Mouse's first on-screen appearance** occurred on this day in 1928. Have the children create and name a cartoon character.

9 The **Gettysburg Address was delivered** on this day in 1863 by Abraham Lincoln. A *score* is equal to 20 years. Have students write other numbers in this form (1 score and 2 years equals 22 years).

Four score and seven years ago...

20 The *United Nations adopted a Declaration of the Rights of the Child* today in 1959. Have students brainstorm a list of what they think should be children's rights.

21 **National Georgia Pecan Month** Bring in pecans to share with the class.

22 **Stop the Violence Day** Brainstorm a list of conflict resolutions. Then, have the class perform short skits illustrating one of these concepts.

23 **Stamp Collecting Month** Invite students to bring in stamps, draw stamps, or give suggestions for images they think should appear on stamps. Compile the information in a class book.

24

I Love Democracy / *I Love Free Speech* / *I Love Religious Freedom*

"What Do You Love About America?" Day Have students write their answers on construction paper flags. Post on a bulletin board.

25 **Marc Brown's Birthday** The children's author and creator of the Arthur Adventure series was born in 1946. Have children illustrate book-marks on 6" x 3" strips of oaktag featuring one of his characters.

26 **Charles Shultz's Birthday** The creator of Charlie Brown and Snoopy was born in 1922. Have the children draw a comic strip featuring a dog.

I'm hungry! | Here is your supper, Buster. | YUM! Good snack! | Now... where is my supper?

27 **No TV Month** Have students brainstorm a list of alternative ways to spend their free time. Challenge them not to watch TV for one evening this month. Have them share their experiences with the class.

28 **International Drum Month** Pass out empty oatmeal containers and coffee cans. Have children use them as drums and play along with recorded music.

29 **Richard E. Byrd made the first flight over the South Pole** on this day in 1929. Teach the class some facts about the South Pole.

30 **Jonathan Swift's Birthday** Born in 1667, he wrote *Gulliver's Travels*. In the story, Gulliver describes a group of tiny people called Lilliputians. Let children illustrate what their rooms at home or their classroom would look like if they were only two or three inches tall.

5

November

Sunday	Monday	Tuesday	Wednesday	Thursday	Friday	Saturday

November Gazette

Teacher _____ Date _____

IN THE NEWS

TAKE NOTE

WHAT'S COMING UP

KID'S CORNER

Unscramble these words.

1. iep _____

2. sarhvet _____

3. krutye _____

4. ogbebl _____

5. setfa _____

Answers: 1. pie 2. harvest 3. turkey 4. gobble 5. feast

Celebrate November!

Dear Family Members,
Here are a few quick-and-easy activities to help you and your child celebrate special days throughout the month of November.

November is *Stamp Collecting Month*

- Help your child make self-sticking stamps. Have him or her draw several small pictures on plain white paper and cut them out. Mix ¼ cup of nontoxic white glue and one tablespoon of vinegar in a plastic container. Paint the backs of the pictures with the glue mixture. Place the pictures face down on a sheet of waxed paper until dry. Attach the stamps by moistening the backs with water.

November is *Peanut Butter Lover's Month*

- Celebrate by making homemade peanut butter with your child using the following recipe:
  - 1½ cups roasted peanuts (unsalted)
  - 1 tablespoon peanut oil

Mix the peanuts and the peanut oil together, then put into a food processor or blender. Process the mixture until it is smooth. Store the peanut butter in a sealed container in the refrigerator. It will keep for two weeks. Enjoy your homemade peanut butter on crackers or apple wedges as a special snack.

November is *No TV Month*

- Talk with your child about different activities to do besides watching television. Make a list of favorite activities. Pick one night each week to be *No TV Night* and do one of the activities on the list instead.

Thanksgiving **is the fourth Thursday in November in the United States**

- Make turkey decorations with your child by painting his or her hand with brown finger paint. Have your child press his or her painted hand onto white paper. When the print has dried, provide markers to add details to the turkeys.

November is *International Creative Child Month*

- Gather items from around the house (buttons, boxes, fabric scraps, wrapping paper, yarn, etc.) and encourage your child to create a unique piece of art from the materials. Display his or her creative efforts in a prominent place.

November 21 is *World Hello Day*

- You and your child can enjoy learning greetings in different languages:
  - French — Bonjour (bohn•ZHOOR)
  - Hebrew — Shalom (sha•LOHM)
  - Italian — Buon giorno (bwohn JOR•noh)
  - Japanese — Konichiwa (koh•NEE•chee•wah)
  - Spanish — Hola (OH•lah)

Read In November!

Dear Family Members,
Here are some books to share with your child to enhance the enjoyment of reading in November.

The Thanksgiving Story by Alice Dalgliesh
- *Follow a pilgrim family as they learn how to live in America and share thanks with their native neighbors.*
- Have your child name something the Pilgrims were thankful for, something the Wampanoags were thankful for, and something he or she is thankful for.

Thanksgiving at Our House by Wendy Watson
- *Tells the story of one family's preparation and celebration of Thanksgiving.*
- Ask your child to draw a picture of a Thanksgiving memory. Then, cut out and decorate a paper frame for the picture.

Across the Wide Dark Sea: The Mayflower Journey by Jean Van Leeuwen
- *Tells of the famous voyage from the point of view of a pilgrim boy sailing to a new land with his family.*
- Have your child name people and things to take if he or she were moving somewhere far away.

Sarah Morton's Day: A Day in the Life of a Pilgrim Girl by Kate Waters
- *Photographs and a first person account of a day in the life of a pilgrim girl at the Plymouth Plantation living museum.*
- Ask your child to tell what a day might be like if he or she were a pilgrim child.

Tapenum's Day: A Wampanoag Indian Boy in Pilgrim Times by Kate Waters
- *Photographs and first person account of a day in the life of a Wampanoag Indian boy at the Hobbamock Homesite at the Plimouth Plantation living museum.*
- Ask your child to tell what a day might be like if he or she were a Wampanoag child.

The Keeping Quilt by Patricia Polacco
- *Follow the life of a family quilt as it is loved and used generation after generation.*
- Share a story about a cherished family heirloom.

The Josefina Story Quilt by Eleanor Coerr
- *A girl stitches a story quilt of her adventures on a wagon trip to California.*
- Have your child glue colored paper squares together and illustrate trips and special memories on them to create a paper quilt.

Gobbling Good Work!

Student

Date

Teacher

© Carson-Dellosa CD-2092

Congratulations Young Author!

Title

Author

Publication Date

© Carson-Dellosa CD-2092

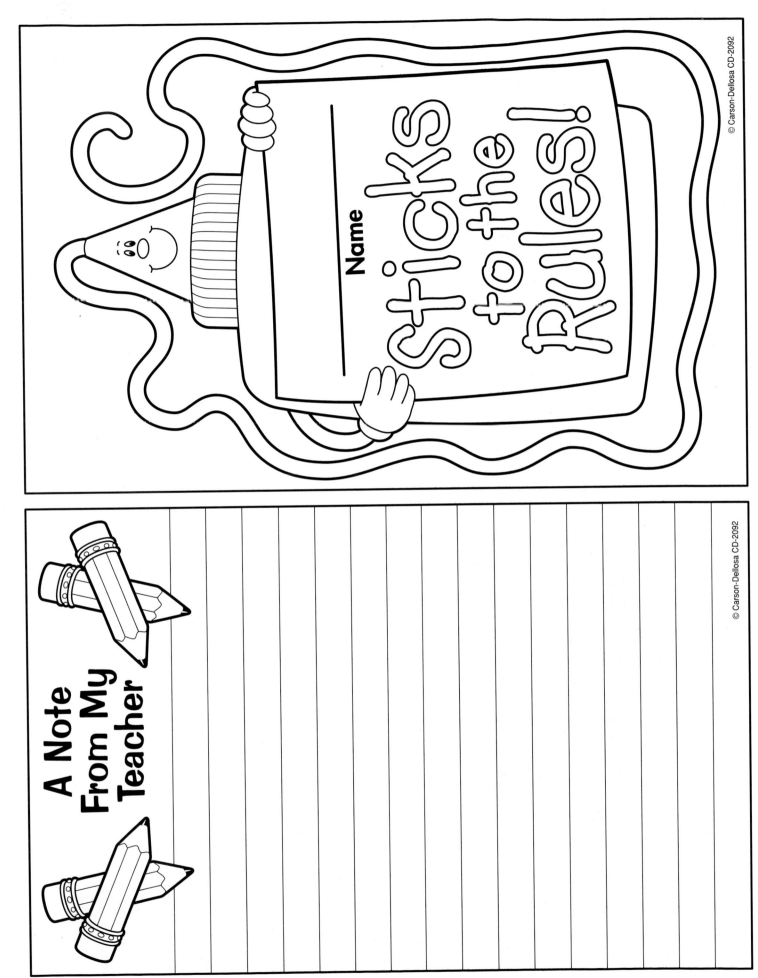

Name _____

Sticks to the Rules!

A Note From My Teacher

NOVEMBER
Writing Activities

Let students feast on a cornucopia of writing activities that will keep their interest levels high all month long.

Say **No** to Turkey

Let students talk turkey! Have students write five reasons for not eating turkey on Thanksgiving from a turkey's point of view. Allow students to share their reasons with the class.

Word Bank Words

turkey	vegetables
frost	wheat
quilt	corn
cornucopia	squash
harvest	pie
thanks	dinner
fruit	feast

Tasty Treats

November is a time to think about favorite foods! Give each student a paper plate. Have them write descriptions of favorite foods on the plates. Post the plates on a bulletin board or wall and let other classmates guess which foods are being described.

My Favorite Food
My favorite food is round and flat. It is made with dough. Some cooks throw it into the air and catch it. Then you put on tomato sauce, meat, and vegetables. Then you cook it and cut it into triangles.

Special Traditions

Have students write about special traditions in their families and their experiences with these traditions, such as *On each family member's birthday, the birthday person gets to wear a paper crown that the rest of the family has decorated.*

Traveling Letters

If you could go anywhere in the world, where would it be? Have each child choose a place he would like to visit and write a letter to a travel bureau or tourist agency asking for information about the destination. Mail the letters and have students use the information received to write a paragraph explaining what they found out.

CHINA

Take a trip down under

AUSTRALIA

Pyramid Poems

Let students show their appreciation for November! Students can follow the instructions to write a pyramid poem about a favorite November subject. Display the poems on a bulletin board titled *November Poems*.

Line 1 is the subject.
Line 2 has two adjectives that describe the subject.
Line 3 has three *-ing* words that describe the subject.
Line 4 is two statements or a statement and a question.

Leaves

red, gold

flying, floating, falling

Rake them into a pile. Jump in!

Different Diaries

Have each student choose a famous person who was born in November, such as Mark Twain, Benjamin Banneker, Marie Curie, Daniel Boone, etc., and write a diary entry reflecting a day in the life of that person.

proofreader's Marks

Mark it! Post a large chart showing several proofreader's marks. Include the symbols (at right) and any others the class is learning. Have children proofread each other's work using red pencils and the proofreader's marks.

⌇	delete
≡	use capital letter
⊙	insert period
lc /	use lowercase
∾	transpose
⌄	insert apostrophe

13

Bulletin Board Ideas

Display good work aplenty with this idea. Cover a bulletin board with any color butcher paper. Cut a large cornucopia shape from brown paper and attach it to the center of the board. Cut large apple, pumpkin, pear, and eggplant shapes from colorful paper, and post them with the cornucopia. Post student papers on the large fruit and vegetable shapes. This display complements the *A Cornucopia of Fall Foods* chapter (pages 20-28).

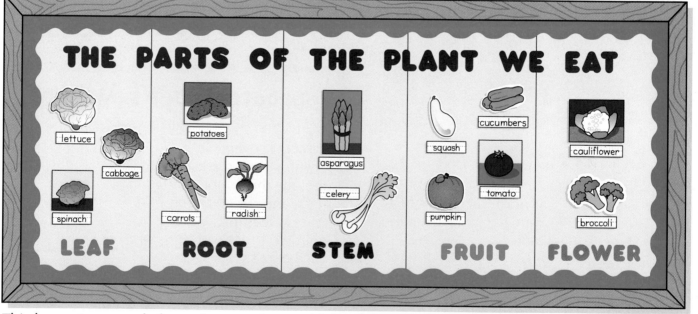

This harvest season, help students understand how different vegetables grow. Cover a bulletin board with colorful paper. Divide the board into five sections labeled *Leaf*, *Root*, *Stem*, *Fruit*, and *Flower*. Have students draw and cut out pictures of vegetables and place them in the appropriate categories. This interactive display may be used with the *A Cornucopia of Fall Foods* chapter (pages 20-28).

14

Reap lots of smiles by displaying student work from your harvest study. Cover the display with seven colors of paper as shown. Cut a large circle from blue construction paper and color in green and white continent shapes. Label six sections with the names of harvest festivals. Have several students write explanations of each celebration and post them with completed crafts or photographs of students participating in activities from the *Harvest Celebrations throughout the World* chapter (pages 29-37).

Cast a vote for student involvement with this balloting bulletin board. Cover the top section with red paper, the middle with white paper, and the bottom with blue paper. Post a question for students to vote on in the middle of the display. Cut a slit in the top of a shoebox and cover the box with colorful paper. Staple the shoebox and an envelope containing copies of the ballot pattern (page 44) to the display. Let students vote on the question by placing their ballots in the voting box. When votes are counted, place a check by the students' choice. This display works well with the *Every Vote Counts* chapter (pages 40-45).

Create a display where classroom authors can place their books for others to read. Cover the bulletin board with colorful paper. Make book holders by cutting off the top third of the front of a manila folder. Staple the bottom and open side of each folder. Personalize each book holder with a student's name and attach it to the board. Let children choose a book they have written to feature in their holders for others to read. Title the display *Mrs. _____'s Authors*. This display is a wonderful complement to the *Classroom Publishing* chapter (pages 46-59).

Encourage reading in your classroom with this display. Cover a bulletin board with colorful paper. Cut out and staple strips of paper to the display to resemble bookshelves. Label sections of the shelves with each child's name. Let students write the titles of books they have read recently on 3"-wide strips of colorful paper and decorate them to look like book spines. Have each student place his "book" on the shelf labeled with his name. Set a goal for a number of books students should read, then reward children with bookmarks when they reach the goal. You may wish to use this bulletin board with the *Classroom Publishing* chapter (pages 46-59).

Create a Thanksgiving display complete with students' thankful thoughts. Cover the bulletin board with colorful paper. Have students draw and cut out self-portraits. Cut pieces of white paper into speech balloons and have each student write about something he is thankful for. Post each speech balloon with the self-portrait. This bulletin board works well with the *Gobbling Good Thanksgiving Fun* chapter (pages 64-72).

Give your students a heaping helping of praise for their best work. Cover a bulletin board with colorful paper. Make a large turkey by cutting a circle from brown paper and attaching it to the center of the board. Cut feather shapes from colorful paper and place them behind the circle. Cut out and color the turkey body pattern (page 70). Cut feet shapes from yellow paper and attach them to the bottom. Post student papers inside the turkey's feathers. Use this display with the *Gobbling Good Thanksgiving Fun* chapter (pages 64-72).

17

A THANKSGIVING FEAST

Sarah   Helen   Erik   Tiffany

Kit   Carter   Whitney

Set a student-designed table for Thanksgiving fun! Cover a bulletin board with colorful paper. Staple a paper tablecloth to the display. Add four strips of brown under the tablecloth to resemble table legs. Give each child a paper plate and have her draw or cut out pictures of Thanksgiving foods to glue to the plate. Use craft glue to attach plastic silverware and napkins to the bulletin board. Attach the plates inside the silverware settings. See *Turkeys Galore Tablecloth* (page 69) for directions to make the turkey handprint border. (Alter the directions by using heavy paper and various colors of paint.) Display this bulletin board during the *Gobbling Good Thanksgiving Fun* chapter (pages 64-72).

Create a Pilgrim village complete with homes and people. Cover the bulletin board with sky- and sea-colored paper. Cut a piece of brown paper to resemble a hillside and attach to the board. Enlarge the Mayflower pattern (page 83) and put it in the "water." Display the pilgrim houses and paper dolls (page 75) on the board to complete the display. This bulletin board is a great complement to *The Pilgrims, the Wampanoag, and the First Thanksgiving* chapter (pages 73-84).

18

Show off the Wampanoag crafts made during your study of *The Pilgrims, the Wampanoag, and the First Thanksgiving* (pages 73-84). Cover the board with colorful paper and divide it into four sections. Display student projects or photographs of projects along with the Wampanoag name for each one.

Design a classroom quilt complete with unique student-designed squares. Give each student a large construction paper square and have him personalize it by drawing things she is thankful for. Create a large classroom quilt by posting the squares on the board, alternating solid squares between them. Use a marker to draw stitch marks between the squares. This display works well with the *Snuggle up with Quilts* chapter (pages 85-92).

A Cornucopia of Fall Foods

Fall brings to mind various types of food since it is the time when many people celebrate harvests. Gather a bountiful harvest of crafts and activities that feature cornucopias, fruits, and vegetables.

DID YOU KNOW?

Before the English settled in America, the word *corn* referred to any type of grain, such as wheat, barley, oats, etc. Then, Native Americans introduced the English to a grain they called *maize*. Because it was a grain, the English called it corn.

The cornucopia, or horn of plenty, is a traditional symbol of the harvest that dates back to Greek mythology. There are several variations of the myth that tell about the cornucopia, but they all involve Zeus giving or receiving a goat's horn. In one version, the horn was filled with fruits and flowers, as we see it today. In another version, the horn would fill with an abundant supply of whatever the owner wanted.

Botanically speaking, a fruit is the edible part of a plant that surrounds the seeds, and a vegetable is any other edible part of the plant (leaves, roots, stem). Following this rule, pumpkins, peppers, and squash, are fruits; lettuce, carrots, and celery are vegetables. However, most people think of fruits as being sweet and vegetables as being savory.

Literature Selections

Harvest Year by Chris Peterson: Boyds Mills Press, Inc., 1996. (Picture book, 32 pg.) Color photographs highlight various foods harvested across the United States each month during the year.

It's a Fruit, It's a Vegetable, It's a Pumpkin by Allan Fowler: Children's Press & Co., 1996. (Science book, 32 pg.) Part of the *Rookie Read-About Science Series*.

Growing Vegetable Soup by Lois Elhert: Harcourt Brace, 1990. (Storybook, 40 pg.) A father and child grow vegetables to make soup.

Jumbo Cornucopia

Create a harvest display of gigantic proportions! Make overgrown fruits and vegetables from papier mâché by mixing a batch of equal parts glue and water (or use papier mâché mix). Dip newspaper strips into the paste and smooth them over inflated balloons, covering them completely. Once the papier mâché is dry, paint the balloons to resemble fruits and vegetables. Roll a sheet of brown butcher paper into a cone shape, staple, and twist up the end. Display the bountiful harvest of fruits and vegetables in the resulting cornucopia.

Horn of Plenty Collage

Create cornucopias that fill with whatever your heart desires. Cut out and color the cornucopia pattern (page 26) and glue to construction paper. Let each child cut pictures of things they want (toys, candy, pets, etc.) from magazines, and glue them "in" and spilling "out" of the cornucopia. Have students write stories about what they would do if they had magic cornucopias and display the stories with the collages.

Cornucopia Mobile

Decorate for the harvest season with spiral cornucopia mobiles.

Step 1
Round the corners of a 9" x 12" sheet of brown construction paper to form an oval. Poke a hole 1" in from the edge, insert scissors and cut a spiral to the center of the oval.

Step 2
Glue colored fruit and vegetable patterns (pages 25,27-28) at the bottom of the intact circle around the outside of the spiral.

Step 3
Punch a hole in the top of the circle and at the tail of the spiral. Tie a string in each hole. Tie the other end of each string to opposite ends of a straw, making the tail string shorter than the circle string.

Step 4
Tie the leftover ends together above the straw to hang the finished craft.

Harvest Still Life

A painting or drawing of an arrangement of inanimate objects is called a still life and is a popular subject for artists. The harvest season provides many colorful fruits and vegetables for still life arrangements. Show students some examples of still life art, then set up an arrangement of fruits and vegetables in a bowl, basket, or cornucopia. Provide art paper, paints and brushes, and let the creative juices flow! Display the finished paintings together beside the real arrangement.

Refrigerator Magnet

Make "attractive" harvest magnets to display throughout the fall. Copy the bread board pattern (page 27) onto brown poster board. Affix several bars of magnetic tape onto the back of the board. Write a happy harvest message on the board and glue on nuts and real wheat (available at craft stores). Before sending the crafts home, use them to display excellent fall work on magnetic boards or file cabinets.

21

Cranberry Bread Recipe and Holder

Cranberries are grown in swampy bogs that are flooded at harvest time. The floating berries are then gathered in large nets and scoops. Send home a recipe for a cranberry harvest treat in a recipe card holder. To make the holder, copy the bread loaf pattern (page 25) twice onto brown paper. Roll small pieces of red tissue paper into balls and glue onto the loaves to resemble cranberries. Glue the loaves onto each side of a clothespin. Write the recipe for Cranberry Bread on the board for students to copy onto note cards. Students can place the recipe cards in the holders and take home to share with their families. For a special treat, let students help make (and eat) the cranberry bread in class!

Cranberry Bread

2 cups sifted all purpose flour
1 cup sugar
1 1/2 teaspoon baking powder
1 teaspoon salt
1/2 teaspoon baking soda
1/4 cup butter or margarine
1 egg, beaten
3/4 cup orange juice
1 teaspoon grated orange peel (optional)
3 cups fresh or frozen cranberries, chopped

Sift flour, sugar, baking powder, salt, and baking soda into a large bowl. Cut in butter until crumbly. Add egg, orange juice, and orange peel and stir until moist. Fold in cranberries. Spoon into a greased 9" x 5" x 3" loaf pan. Bake at 350° for 1 hour.

Three Sisters Mosaic

The Iroquois and other eastern Native Americans referred to corn, beans, and squash (including pumpkins) as the Three Sisters. These crops were important to the Native Americans because they grew very well and made for a bountiful harvest. Create beautiful mosaic designs with these Native American harvest foods. Draw a design on a sheet of heavy black paper, such as a pumpkin or sunflower, or a geometric pattern. Glue on popcorn kernels, pumpkin seeds, and a variety of dried beans, filling in the design with color and texture.

A-"Maize"-ing Colors

Indian corn comes in a variety of colors, including red, yellow, orange, white, black, and blue. Make 3-dimensional maize that shows off these harvest colors. Trim 3" from a long cardboard tube and let students use markers to draw multi-colored corn kernels in rows along the tube. Cut out four cornhusks from a brown paper bag and glue to one end of the tube. Tape bunches of raffia around the inside of the other end of the tube to resemble cornsilk.

22

Pumpkins On the Vine

Pumpkins are harvested for a variety of uses including jack o'lanterns, baking, and decorating. Make a decorative string of pumpkins that can be displayed on a table, or hung like a garland.

Step 1 Hold a 9" x 12" sheet of orange construction paper horizontally and cut into strips, approximately ¹/₂" wide. Criss-cross four strips and glue them together, dotting glue between each layer at the intersection of the strips.

Step 2 When dry, lift each strip, one at a time, and glue the ends together, forming a pumpkin shape. One sheet of orange paper should yield four pumpkins.

Step 3 Cut four small pumpkin leaves and four short, thin strips from green paper. Curl the thin strips and glue one leaf and one curled strip to the top of each pumpkin. Cut a brown lunch bag, around in a spiral from the top, creating one long strip of brown paper. Twist the strip to look like a vine and thread through each pumpkin, or use green curling ribbon to form the vine and tendrils.

"Gourd"-geous Creations

Gourds are similar to squash, but are inedible. Throughout history, gourds have been harvested for a variety of uses including musical instruments, bowls, spoons, and water containers. The gourds are dried, hollowed out, and painted with intricate designs. Turn fresh gourds into works of art by painting them with acrylic paint to look like faces or animals, following the shape of the gourd to creatively form the features. Fresh gourds will only last for a couple of weeks before the paint becomes distorted. To dry gourds before painting, poke a thick wire through the neck to create a loop for hanging. Let the gourds hang for 4-6 weeks in a dry place, until you can hear the seeds rattle inside. Scrub with a brush to remove any mildew, buff with a cloth, and then paint.

Agricultural Product Map

Many crops are harvested throughout the United States. Use encyclopedias and other reference books to determine where certain crops are grown, then make product maps. Let each child pick four or five crops and create his own symbols for each. Color the symbols on a map pattern (page 26) in the appropriate regions and create a map key for the symbols at the bottom. Write several harvest questions that can be answered using the map, such as *Where are apples harvested?* Students can exchange maps and questions with a partner.

23

Homemade Raisins

Explain to students that before people had refrigerators and freezers, they had to find ways to keep fruits and vegetables from spoiling. Drying, canning, and making preserves continue to be popular food-preservation methods. Dry seedless grapes to make homemade raisins. Grapes must be prepared before drying by cracking the skin. Crack the skin by plunging grapes into boiling water for 30 seconds, then plunging into cold water to stop the cooking process. Let them drain on paper towels. Place the grapes on a greased cooling rack on top of a cookie sheet, and place in an oven, preheated to 140°. Leave the oven door ajar and dry for 30-60 minutes, periodically testing for doneness.

Fruits and Cornucopia

Harvest a quick and easy snack that's sure to please. Make cornucopia snack holders by rolling paper plates into cone shapes. Staple to secure, then twist and curve up the bottom of the cone. Make the snack mix by combining cone-shaped corn snacks and fruit shaped cereal. Let students scoop up the snack mix with their paper plate cornucopias and enjoy!

Cross-Section Garden

In a vegetable garden you might see pumpkins, squash, and lettuce, but where are the carrots, potatoes and radishes? Underground! Bring all the vegetables in the garden into view with this cross section garden picture. Cut a sheet of green and a sheet of brown construction paper in half, vertically. Glue the green paper together end to end, forming a long strip and repeat with the brown paper. Then, glue the green strip (above ground) to the top of the brown strip (below ground). Color and cut out several vegetable patterns (pages 25, 27-28), including some that grow above ground and some that grow below ground. Glue each vegetable to the paper in the appropriate place. Label the vegetables and display in one long strip along a wall to create a class garden.

Harvest Soup

Warm up with a cup of harvest soup! Heat two cans vegetable or chicken broth in a crock pot and add a variety of fresh, canned, and frozen vegetables, including canned tomatoes and corn, chopped celery and carrots, and frozen peas and green beans. Add salt and pepper to taste. Let the soup simmer for several hours before serving. After eating the soup, write the recipe on the board and let students copy it onto the lined side of a 5" x 7" note card. Students can illustrate the backs of the cards with pictures of the ingredients, the process, or the finished products.

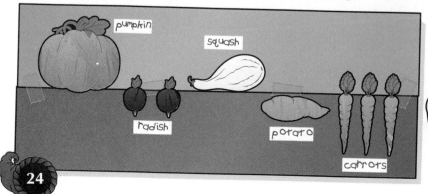

24

COPY and CUT

pumpkin

bread loaf

radish

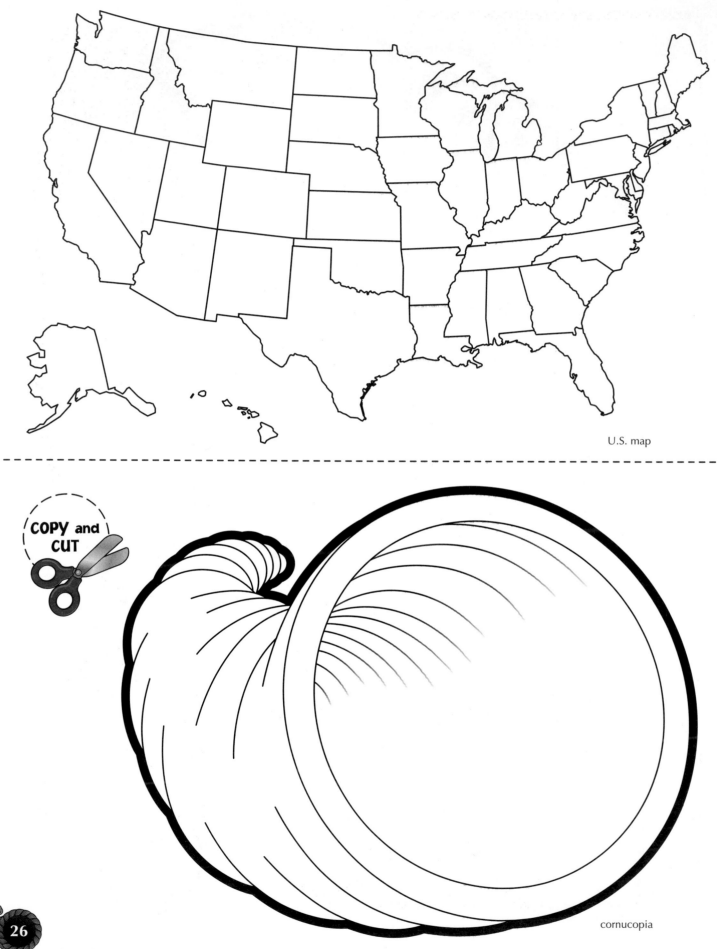

U.S. map

COPY and CUT

cornucopia

26

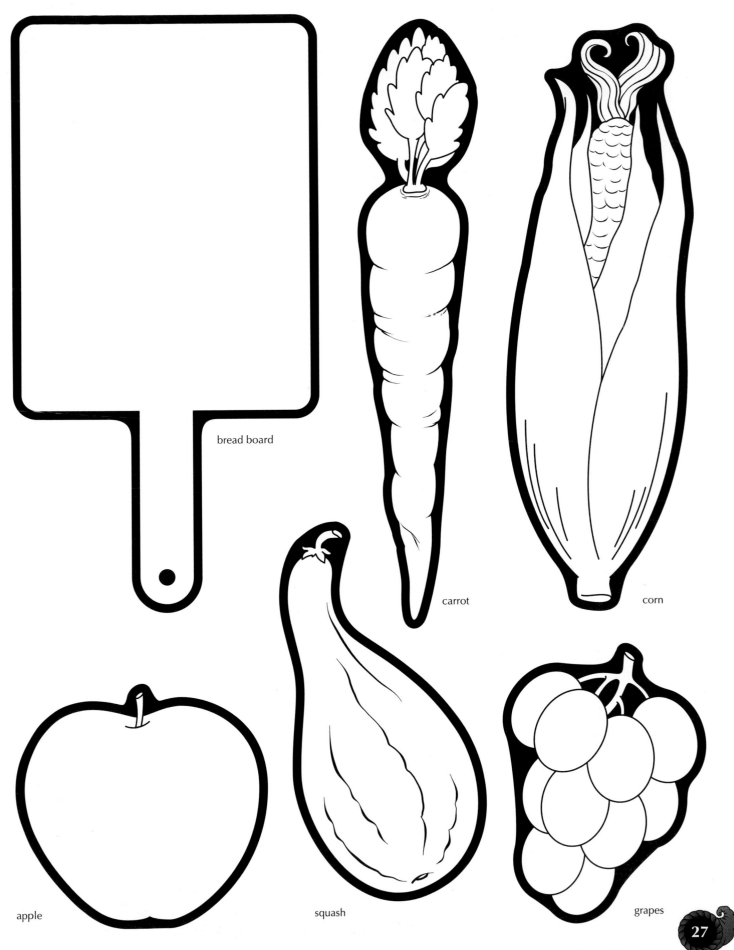

bread board

carrot

corn

apple

squash

grapes

27

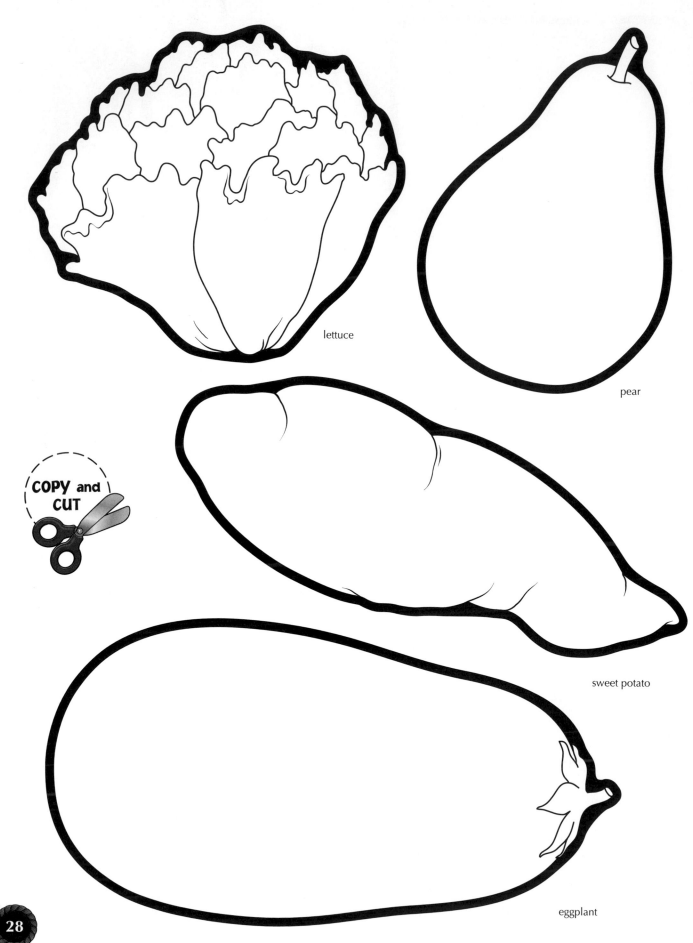

lettuce

pear

COPY and CUT

sweet potato

eggplant

Harvest Celebrations throughout the World

After the hard work of harvesting crops, people all over the world celebrate with festivals, food, and fun. While the times of harvest festivals vary in different parts of the world, November is a good time to acquaint students with the diverse ways that people all over the world live, harvest, and celebrate!

Did You Know?

- The ancient Greeks and Romans celebrated the harvest by offering newly-harvested foods to the goddess of corn—*Demeter* to the Greeks and *Ceres* to the Romans.
- Many past cultures believed that spirits lived inside corn and made it grow. Egyptians would cry when they harvested the corn to show the spirits that they were sorry for cutting down the stalks.
- In England, it was thought that the corn spirit hopped from corn stalk to corn stalk, and that the corn spirit was trapped in the last stalk. This last stalk was often made into a doll that was used in rituals to ensure a good harvest the next year.
- To many Native American tribes, the *Green Corn Ceremony* marked the beginning of a new year.

Literature Selections

Itse Selu: Cherokee Harvest Festival by Daniel Pennington: Charlesbridge Publishing, 1994. (Illustrated storybook, 32 pg.) Follow a Cherokee family through their preparations for and celebration of the Green Corn Ceremony.

The Moon Lady by Amy Tan: Macmillan Publishing Company, 1992. (Storybook, 32 pg.) A grandmother tells her granddaughters about celebrating the Harvest Moon Festival in China when she was young.

The Wind and the Sukkah by Aydel Lebovics: Merkos Linyonei Chinuch, 1990. (Storybook, 32 pg.) The wind brings needed materials to a man building a Sukkah for the Jewish harvest celebration, Sukkoth.

Harvest Festivals Around the World by Judith Hoffman Corwin: Julian Messner, 1995. (Informational book, 48 pg.) Emphasizes ancient civilizations and indigenous peoples and includes 15 activities, such as recipes, masks, dolls, paper flowers, hieroglyphics, and other crafts.

Sukkoth

Sukkoth (SOO-kot) is a Jewish Holiday that celebrates the harvest. Sukkoth is called the Festival of Booths because it recalls the time the Jewish people wandered in the desert for forty years, living in temporary shelters, and also the Jewish farming tradition of living in huts in the field during harvest. To celebrate Sukkoth, special plants are gathered; a booth, or *sukkah* (SOO-kah), is built and decorated; and a feast is enjoyed in the sukkah.

Build A Sukkah

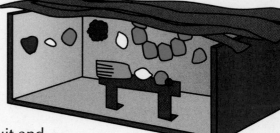

A sukkah is made from temporary walls and includes a roof made from loose branches that provide shade but allow the stars to show through at night, reminding the Jewish people of the days when their ancestors dwelt in temporary shelters. Make a 3-dimensional sukkah from a shoe box. Have an adult cut one long side of the box out with scissors or a craft knife. Cut out a table with two legs from brown paper and fruit and vegetable shapes from colored paper. Glue some fruits and vegetables to the walls and some to the table. Bend back the legs of the table at the bottom and tape the resulting flaps to the bottom of the box. Cut long, thin strips of brown paper and glue across the top of the booth, leaving spaces in between. Display the sukkah during Sukkoth.

Harvest Garland

During Sukkoth, the walls and ceiling of a sukkah are decorated with garlands of harvest fruits and vegetables. It was believed that even though the sukkah was a temporary home, it should be as beautiful and comfortable to live in as a permanent home. Create harvest garlands to use for decorations during the harvest season. Cut out and color fruit and vegetable patterns (pages 25, 27-28) and tape them in a pattern to a length of string or ribbon.

Lulav Centerpiece

Four special plants are gathered during Sukkoth as a symbol of God's bounty. Palm, myrtle, and willow branches are bound together with palm leaves into a bunch called the *lulav* (LOO-lauv). The lulav is paraded through the synagogue in a ceremony of thanks along with the fourth special plant, an etrog (or citron). Make a lulav centerpiece with paper leaves. Cover a tall potato chip can with brown construction paper and add "palm" leaves (cut strips of dark green paper into long, palm leaf shapes). Cut out several willow and myrtle leaf patterns (page 37) and glue them onto long strips of brown poster board. Arrange the branches in the container along with a few extra "palm" leaves. If possible, show pictures of the plants or bring in actual samples for the class to view.

Green Corn Ceremony

Many Native American tribes celebrate the corn crop before the harvest work is done. A Green Corn Ceremony (also called Green Corn Festival and Green Corn Dance) is held when the corn becomes ripe, to thank the spirits for the corn harvest. Traditions vary from tribe to tribe, but usually the celebration lasts for several days and includes games, story-telling, ceremonial dances, and a big feast. People celebrating the festival are forbidden to eat the new corn before official prayers have been offered to the spirits.

Ball Game

Several Native American tribes play a game with a pole and a ball during the Green Corn Festival. The object of the game is to throw a small ball at a pole and hit it at the highest point. Display a strip of brown paper vertically on a wall. Allow students to take turns throwing a small bean bag ball at the "pole" and marking where the ball hit with their name. See who can throw the ball highest on the "pole."

Green Corn Invitation

When the corn was almost ripe, a Cherokee high chief would send a message to the villages, inviting them to a Green Corn Ceremony. Each village would then send back an ear of green corn to accept the invitation. Make corn-shaped invitations to a Green Corn Ceremony and "peel" back the green husks to reveal the message inside. Let each child draw an ear of corn on yellow paper and cut out. Draw two corn husk shapes that are slightly larger than the corn shape. Overlap the green husk pieces and place on top of the yellow corn. Fasten the layers together with a paper fastener at the base of the corn. Slide the husks to the sides and write an invitation to an imaginary Green Corn Ceremony on the yellow corn. Have students include information about what might occur at the ceremony based on what they have learned.

You are invited to a Green Corn Ceremony

Peach Stone Game

At the end of the Green Corn Ceremony, some Native Americans play a game of chance with painted peach pits. Paint peach pits blue on one side and red on the other side. Assign a value to each color, for example, red = 2 and blue = 5. Place the pits in a plastic container with a lid and shake them. Empty the peach pits onto a table. Count up points based on which sides the pits land (2 blue and 2 red would equal 14 points). Let pairs of students take turns shaking and emptying the container until one player's score reaches 100. (If peach pits are not available, use 3-4 small, flat rocks.

31

Harvest Moon Festival

In mid-Autumn, the full moon is considered to be at its biggest and brightest. During this time, the moon is called a harvest moon because the bright moon enables farmers to harvest into the night. The Chinese say this time marks the birthday of the moon. The Chinese Harvest Moon Festival celebrates the rice and wheat harvests and commemorates the legend of Chang-O, a woman who flew to the moon and can still be seen when it is full.

Flowers from the Moon

It was once believed in China that during the Harvest Moon Festival, flowers would fall from the moon and that good luck would come to those who saw them. Let students make good luck moon cards to celebrate the harvest moon. Cut out two yellow circles and tape them together to form a card. Tape several strands of yarn inside the card and tape a flower cut from paper to the end of each strand. Write messages of good luck and happy harvest on each flower, then gather and place the flowers and yarn inside the card. When cards are opened, lucky flowers will fall from the moon card.

Moon Cakes

Moon cakes are the traditional food to eat and exchange with friends and family during the Harvest Moon Festival. Moon cakes are yellow and round like the full moon, made with nuts or a bean paste, and are often stamped with a picture of a hare. According to legend, the Chinese won an important battle because of notes baked into moon cakes that told troops about the time of attack. Have students write secret messages, with nontoxic pens or markers, on the insides of paper cupcake liners. Place a second liner inside the first and bake. Cover cupcakes with light yellow frosting and sprinkle with sugar. Let students exchange moon cakes and read their secret messages.

The Lady In the Moon

In China, the man in the moon is seen as a woman or a hare. Let students interpret what they see in the moon with this full moon craft. Cut a circle of poster board for each student and let her draw a simple picture on the circle of what she sees in the moon. Trace over the lines with glue, lay heavy string along the glue pattern, and let dry. Crumple and unfold a sheet of aluminum foil. Paint a thin layer of glue over the circle and string, and carefully press the foil (shiny side up) onto the circle, pressing around the string. Fold and glue the excess foil around the back of the circle. Patch tears with extra foil and let dry. Mix two parts yellow paint with one part water and paint over the foil. Gently rub over the picture with a paper towel, leaving the paint in the creases.

Homowo

The Ga people of the west African nation of Ghana mock an ancient famine each year at harvest time with their festival, *Homowo*, which means *to hoot at hunger*. The celebration lasts for three days. People spend time with family, honor their ancestors, and enjoy a large feast of freshly harvested foods, including soups made from yam, corn, or palm. *Kpekpele* is a traditional food eaten during the harvest celebration in Ghana. It is made from corn meal and palm oil. On the last day of Homowo, the chief ruler of the Ga people walks through the town sprinkling kpekpele in the air to honor their Ga ancestors.

Twins Party

During Homowo, twins and triplets are honored as special gifts from God. Twins and triplets are decorated with body paints and are served special foods made from yams. Allow children to talk about any twins or triplets they know at school or in their families. Have students write and decorate special letters to these people that inform them of the special status of twins during this African festival.

Yam Festival Snack

The yam is a common vegetable grown in west Africa and is a major part of the Homowo festival. Mashed yams with hard boiled eggs is often made for ceremonies or celebrations, such as the yam festival for twins during Homowo. Yams are root vegetables and are similar to potatoes. Let students explore yams by comparing them to potatoes. In small groups, examine yams and potatoes and outline their physical differences. Provide small bowls of mashed yams and mashed potatoes for students to taste and compare.

Kente Cloth

During Homowo, people can be seen wearing brightly colored kente cloth draped over their shoulders as a kind of toga. Kente cloth is woven with bright colors in geometric patterns. Weaving kente cloth is a traditional craft in Ghana. Let students create unique kente cloth patterns of their own. Let each child divide a sheet of white paper into nine sections. Draw the same geometric pattern (stripes, zigzags, triangles, etc.) in every other section on the page (in the four corners and the middle) and color them all the same. Pick a different pattern to draw in the remaining sections, coloring them all the same as well. Display the kente cloths on a background of black paper.

Pongal

The monsoon season in India provides ideal conditions to make India the world's second largest producer of rice. The fields remain flooded until the end of the growing season. At harvest, the stalks are cut, tied in bundles, and left in the sun to dry. In southern India, the rice harvest is celebrated with a sweet, sticky rice mixture. Because of the many languages spoken, the mixture has many names, but in the state of Tamil, it is called *Pongal*, which is also the name of the four-day-long rice harvest celebration. Offers are made to the gods and the birds (a symbol of beauty), houses are cleaned and decorated, and cows are honored for their hard work during the harvest.

Kolam

A design called a *Kolam* is drawn on the floor with rice powder before Pongal begins. The designs often represent the sun in honor of the sun's role in the harvest. The Pongal pot is placed in a special spot inside the Kolam, facing the east towards the sun. Let students make a Kolam on brown paper by smearing white powdered tempera paint in sun designs onto the paper. Cut out a pot pattern (page 37) from black paper and glue it onto the Kolam design. Glue grains of rice "boiling" over at the top of the pot.

Thanks to Cows

One day during the four-day Pongal festival is devoted to honoring cows for their work pulling plows in the rice fields. Cows are washed and decorated. Their horns are painted bright colors and garlands of flowers and bells are draped around their necks. Students can depict this custom by creating these decorative cards. Cut out the cow pattern (page 37), draw decorations on it, and color the horns. Tear small pieces of colorful tissue paper. Wrap each piece around the point of a pencil, dip in glue and place in a row around the cow's neck, creating a flower garland. Glue the cow onto a folded piece of paper and write a note of thanks to cows, thanking them for giving us milk and helping farmers plow the fields. Finish the card by gluing a small bell under the flower garland.

Pongal Snack

The word *pongal* literally means *to boil*. Pongal is made from milk, sugar, and rice. It is shared with family, friends, the gods, and animals. As the large pot of Pongal starts to boil, people yell, "Pongal, Pongal!" Make a pot of rice pudding, similar to Pongal, and share it with your class. To make rice pudding for 12, boil 5 cups of milk. Then, stir in 2 cups instant rice, 1 teaspoon of salt, 1/2 teaspoon cinnamon, 1/2 teaspoon nutmeg, and 2/3 cup sugar and cover. Boil for five minutes and reduce heat to low. Mix 4 eggs with 1 cup milk and 1 teaspoon vanilla and add to the rice mixture. Cover, stirring occasionally until thick (about 20 minutes).

34

Maple Sugar Festivals

Maple sugar festivals are held right after *sugaring time* in communities all over southeast Canada and the northeastern United States. Sugaring time comes when the temperature at night sometimes drops below freezing and the days grow warmer. Sunlight and warmth cause the sap to begin to flow within the tree. The maple sap is "harvested" by hammering a tap into the trunk of a maple tree and collecting the sweet sap in buckets hung below the taps. The maple sugar is then boiled to make maple syrup and maple candy.

The Real Thing

Celebrate sugaring time in the sweetest possible way—have a taste test! Create shaped pancakes by pouring pancake batter into maple leaf-shaped cookie cutters on a hot griddle. Serve the pancakes, first with 100% natural maple syrup and then with the artificially flavored type. Let each child choose a favorite and then graph the results. Discuss the meanings of the words *natural* and *artificial* and have the class name other things that fall into these categories.

Sugarbush

A forest of maple trees where sap is collected is called a *sugarbush*. Create a sugarbush in the classroom and let each child contribute a tree to the forest. Ask students to draw and cut out tree shapes from large brown construction paper and display them together on a bulletin board. Then, paint small paper cups with gray paint and use push pins (as taps) to attach the paper cups (buckets) to the tree trunks. Title the display, *It's Sugaring Time!*

Pancake Flipping Relay

Pancakes are a common find at a maple sugar festival. Stacks of pancakes are served with fresh maple syrup. Pancake flipping contests are also held at many festivals. Divide the class into two teams and see which team can flip the fastest. Tape black paper griddles to two desks and draw lines 2-3 yards back from each desk. Cut circles from craft foam for the pancakes. Line up each team behind a line and give the first child on each team a rubber pancake spatula with a "pancake" on it. Each child on the team must flip the pancake from the spatula onto the griddle, scoop it up, and give it to the next child in line.

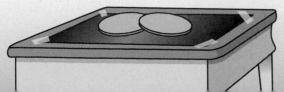

35

Harvest Festivals Around the United States

Harvest festivals are popular in towns all over the United States. The crop that has been harvested may vary from region to region, but certain festivities and events are common in all areas. Harvest festivals center around communities, food, and fun and often include hay rides, music, crafts, and games. Pumpkins and apples are typical themes for harvest festivals in the United States.

Swing Your Partner

Harvest festivals often include square dancing. Square dancing was popular in farming areas where it was often done to celebrate a barn raising. Limber up while having fun with a few easy square dance steps. Have groups of four students form squares, with one student in each corner, pairs facing each other. Teach students to bow to their partner, swing their partner (walk, arm in arm, in a clockwise circle) and dosido (arms folded, walk forward, past your partner, step to the side and walk backwards, past your partner again, returning to your original spot.) Play recorded music and call the different steps. When students learn the basics, introduce other steps such as promenade (walking together in a big clockwise circle) and swing your corner (like swing your partner, but with the person in the opposite corner of the square).

Pumpkin Rolling Contest

Make a class pumpkin patch! Cut out pumpkins and decorate the classroom to look like a pumpkin patch. Then, have a pumpkin rolling contest outside or in a multipurpose room. Let students take turns rolling real medium sized pumpkins to see how far they roll. Measure the distances and write students' names and the distances on the paper pumpkins.

Pumpkin Cupcakes

Celebrate the bounty of the harvest with your class by serving warm apple cider and pumpkin cupcakes. If desired, students could help prepare the snack and then share the treats with the office or cafeteria staff.

Pumpkin Cupcakes

Preheat oven to 325º. Grease or paper-line 16 muffin cups. Combine one 16-ounce package pound cake mix, 2 eggs, 1 cup canned pumpkin, 1/3 cup water, 2 teaspoons pumpkin pie spice, and 1 teaspoon baking soda in a large mixing bowl. Beat on medium speed for 3 minutes. Pour batter into prepared muffin cups, filling 3/4 full. Bake for 25 to 30 minutes or until wooden pick inserted in center comes out clean. Cool in pans on wire racks for 10 minutes. Remove to wire racks to cool completely. Spread cupcakes with prepared vanilla frosting.

COPY and CUT

cow

pot

myrtle leaf

willow leaf

37

A Touch of Frost

Welcome chilly weather with these Jack Frost activities.

Did You Know?

* The story of Jack Frost may have originated in Scandinavia. *Kari*, the god of the winds in Norse mythology, had a son named *Jokul Frosti*. In some Scandian languages, the word *Jokul* means icicle and *Frosti* means frost.
* In Russia, frost is depicted as an old man called Father Frost who holds the Earth and oceans captive with his chains.
* Old Mother Frost often represents frost in German tales. As the story goes, Old Mother Frost shakes out her bed, causing white feathers (snow) to fly about.

Literature Selections

* ***Here Comes Jack Frost*** by Sharon Peters: Troll Associates, 1981. (Picture book, 32 pg.) On a chilly autumn evening, Jack Frost appears and decorates windows with pretty patterns.

* ***Jack Frost & the Magic Paint Brush*** by Kathy Darling: Garrand Publishing Company, 1985. (Picture book, 32 pg.) Jack Frost frolics through the autumn evening using his paint brush to add a glow to outdoor objects.

Portraits of Jack Frost

Jack Frost is an imaginary character who supposedly signals the approach of cold weather by creating shimmering, delicate patterns on windows and other objects. Jack Frost is often depicted as an elf-like character who carries a paintbrush which he uses to paint frosty swirls and designs. Challenge children to draw pictures of what they think Jack Frost looks like. Allow students to enhance their artwork using clear glitter, cotton balls, and fabric scraps.

Old Jack Frost Song

(Sing to the tune of *This Old Man*.)

Old Jack Frost,
Plays with ice,
Paints my window
Oh so nice.
Frosty patterns shimmer
Bright and new.
Winter's near,
I know it's true.

A Frosty Experiment

Create frost in any season with this experiment. Fill a coffee can $2/3$ full with crushed ice. Fill the rest of the can with salt. Stir the ice and salt together gently. Spread $1/2$ teaspoon of water onto a sheet of paper. Place the can of ice and salt on top of the paper. Allow the can to sit for 5-10 minutes or until frost begins forming on the outside of the can. Use a magnifying glass to observe the formations. Explain that frost formed on the can because the moist air from the damp paper adhered to the can and froze. Real frost forms when the temperature outside is low enough to freeze the moisture in the air, coating the ground and other surfaces.

Frosted Windows

Try to duplicate the work of Jack Frost with frosty window designs using an Epsom salt wash. Begin by having students cut out window shapes from pieces of light blue construction paper. Make the wash by mixing one part Epsom salt to two parts hot (not boiling) water until dissolved. When the mixture is cool, let students use it to paint their windows. Cut out curtains for the window from fabric or wallpaper scraps and glue them around the edges of the window. When dry, display the frosty window designs around the classroom.

The Story of Jack Frost

Let students write stories about Jack Frost using one of the story prompts below. Display each student's story along with his illustration from *Portraits of Jack Frost* (page 38).

During the day, Jack Frost hides…

If I were Jack Frost, people would know winter was coming because…

Jack Frost spends his summers…

Frost on the Pumpkin

Frost will be on the pumpkin, grass, and everything else in these sparkling scenes. Have students draw and color outdoor autumn scenes on construction paper. Then, have students use a thin layer of white paint to coat the grass and other objects. When dry, brush a thin coat of glue onto the paint and then sprinkle with clear glitter. Watch the pictures shimmer just as actual frost does on a sunny fall morning.

39

EVERY ✓OTE COUNTS!

Speeches, campaign posters, and the anticipation of who will win—these are all part of Election Day. In the United States, national elections are held on the first Tuesday after the first Monday in November, along with many state and local elections. Students can begin to learn about the democratic process by engaging in these fun classroom activities!

Did You Know?

- The word *ballot* comes from the Italian word *ballotta*. Hundreds of years ago, a person voting in Italy would cast a secret vote using a little colored ball called a *ballotta*.
- Originally, voters in the American colonies had to travel to their colony's capital to vote. Because this could be a long and sometimes dangerous journey, people began to vote locally. A horseback rider then carried the results to each capital to be counted.

Literature Selections

The Vote: Making Your Voice Heard by Linda Scher: Raintree/Steck-Vaughn, 1996. (Informational book, 48 pg.) Discusses who can vote, who does vote, where to vote, and how to vote wisely.

Voting and Elections by Dennis Fradin: Children's Press, 1985. (Informational book, 48 pg.) A brief history of voting and an explanation of election procedures in the United States.

The History of Voting

Throughout history people have voted, but in different ways. In ancient Greece, a vote was cast by dropping either a white or black stone into a box. Long ago in England, people voted verbally. Each voter would call out the name of the person he wanted to elect and his choice would be recorded. People in Australia voted by secret ballot. The names of the candidates were printed on a piece of paper and each voter marked his ballot in a private booth. Experiment by having children vote using each method. First, ask a yes or no question such as "Do you like ice cream?" and let children vote verbally. Next, ask another yes or no question and have children vote by dropping a light dried bean (yes) or a dark dried bean (no) into a shoe box with an opening cut in the top. Last, vote by secret ballot using the ballot pattern (page 44). Write a question on the board with several choices and let students vote by marking their choice and dropping the ballots into the shoe box. Have students compare the different methods and talk about possible reasons why people vote in elections today using secret ballots.

VOTE!

Voting Booth

Explain that people vote in closed booths so they can cast secret ballots. Create a voting booth by cutting out one side of a large appliance box, leaving approximately 12" of cardboard at the top. Provide red, white, and blue paper and markers for students to decorate the outside of the booth. Cut a slit in the box panel opposite the door through which students place their ballots. Attach a large grocery bag underneath the outside opening to hold the ballots. Make a curtain for the voting booth by taping lengths of red, white, and blue streamers to the cardboard overhang above the doorway. Put a chair or small table inside the booth. Choose a student to sit outside the voting booth. As children vote, have the student give them a copy of the ballot pattern (page 44), then check off their names from a class list of voters, ensuring each person votes only one time. Stage a class election using the ideas in *Cast Your Vote* (below).

☑ Cast Your Vote

Provide a classroom-related topic on which the class can vote, such as a game to play at recess. Then, have students cast their ballots in the *Voting Booth* (above). Assign an election committee to collect and tally the votes after the poll has closed. Let an election committee member pass out copies of the *I Voted!* badge pattern (page 45) for voters to color, cut out, and tape to their shirts to let schoolmates know they participated in your class election.

Election Cake

In colonial America, Election Day was celebrated by lighting bonfires, ringing bells, and blowing whistles. Special dinners and picnics were prepared, complete with a fruit and nut election cake. Carry on the election cake tradition with students by bringing in a cake with the word *Vote* written using red, white, and blue candies. After children have voted in an election (as in *Cast Your Vote* above), treat them to a piece of sweet election cake.

The Right Stuff

Political candidates use advertisements to inform voters about themselves and what they will do if elected. Let each student create a poster which lists what he will do if elected president. Display these posters around your classroom. Then, let each student give a short speech about the statements on his poster.

Vote for Jonathan!

"I promise to put a playground in every neighborhood!"

Cast Your Vote Song

(Tune: *If You're Happy and You Know It*)
If you want to cast your vote, raise your hand.
If you want to cast your vote, say yea or nay.

There are many ways to vote,
Don't be late and miss the boat.
On Election Day be sure to cast your vote.

If you want to cast your vote, check the box.
If you want to cast your vote, punch the card.

There are many ways to vote,
Don't be late and miss the boat.
On Election Day be sure to cast your vote.

Take Me to Your Leaders

Citizens vote to elect not only presidents, but also mayors and governors. Explain that people elect a governor to oversee their state and a mayor to oversee their city or town. Familiarize students with the people who hold these offices in their communities. Have each child cut out a simple outline of the United States from a sheet of 11" x 17" paper. Then, students should enlarge and cut out an outline of their state from a 9" x 12" sheet of paper. Cut out a star shape to represent the city or town. Glue the state on the country, and glue the star to the appropriate place on the state. Write the name of the president on the country, the name of the governor on the state, and the name of the mayor on the star.

New York Governor

N.Y. City Mayor

New York

Which symbol is your favorite?

Sally

Tom

Hal

Nancy

Jeff

Megan

The Donkey and the Elephant

In 1947, Thomas Nast, a political cartoonist, published a cartoon that depicted the Republican party as an elephant. Soon the elephant became the official symbol of the party. Later, he drew a donkey to symbolize the Democratic party. Today the elephant and donkey continue to be the symbols of these two American political parties. Copy and cut out the donkey and elephant patterns (page 45). Use the symbols to create a graph where students vote on the symbol they like best.

42

Who's In Charge?

Different parts of a community are overseen by different elected officials. To help children understand which people are elected to what positions, create a matching game using the *Who's in Charge?* game pattern (page 44). Let students color and cut out the game pattern and glue it to poster board. Punch holes as shown beside each office and community. Cut a length of blue yarn and tape one end to the back of the poster board. Wrap clear tape around the opposite end of the yarn so it can be easily threaded through the holes. Have students match each elected office to the appropriate community by threading the yarn through the correct holes. Include a small answer key on the back of the game board for self-checking.

EVERY VOTE COUNTS!

WHO'S IN CHARGE?

Country   Mayor

State   President

City or Town   Governor

Majority Rules

Explain that after the votes in an election have been counted, the person or choice with the *majority* of the votes is the winner. Help children understand the term majority using classroom themes. Determine whether there is a majority of boys or girls in the class, which year the majority of the students were born, and whether the majority of students are right-handed or left-handed. Write the categories on chart paper, along with the number of students for each. Students can use the information to write sentences describing the classroom majority. Combine the completed sentences into a book titled *Our Classroom Majorities*.

What's Your Opinion?

Public opinion polls are used to find out what a sampling of the public thinks. Encourage students to act as pollsters and conduct an opinion poll at home. Choose a question and give voters two choices. Older students may conduct the poll at school. Combine the information into a pictograph or bar graph.

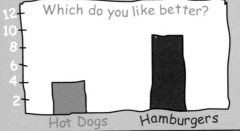

Family Opinion Poll

Which do you like better?

12
10
8
6
4
2

Hot Dogs   Hamburgers

Toss In Your Hat!

Give new meaning to the phrase *throwing your hat into the ring* with this game. Explain that when a person decides to run for an elected office, it is said that he is *throwing his hat into the ring*. Create a class hat tossing game by placing a large hoop or masking tape circle in an open area and have students take turns tossing a hat or cap into the ring from different distances.

43

BALLOT

☐ _____

☐ _____

☐ _____

WHO'S IN CHARGE?

Country ●   ● Mayor

State ●   ● President

City or Town ●   ● Governor

COPY and CUT

elephant

I VOTED!

I Voted! badge

donkey

45

© Carson-Dellosa CD-2092

CLASSROOM PUBLISHING

Literature Selections

Author: A True Story by Helen Lester: Houghton Mifflin Company, 1997. (Picture book, 32 pg.) A children's book writer tells about her childhood experiences with writing and how she became an author as an adult.

From Pictures to Words by Janet Stevens: Holiday House, 1995. (Picture book, 28 pg.) Joined by her own characters, an author describes the process involved in writing, illustrating, and publishing a children's book.

If You Were a Writer by Joan Lowery Nixon: Aladdin Paperbacks, 1995. (Picture book, 28 pg.) A curious daughter learns from her mother, who is a writer, how to find ideas and turn them into interesting and exciting stories.

Read! Read!
Read! Read!

Read a Good Book Today!

Celebrate Children's Book Week

National Children's Book Week is celebrated annually in the United States during the week before Thanksgiving. Spark interest in reading while encouraging students to become *published* classroom authors using these reading, writing, publishing, and book-making ideas!

Did You Know?

- The earliest known books were made of symbols carved into clay tablets.

- Egyptians used a plant called *papyrus* to make a paper-like substance. They pasted sheets of pounded papyrus together to make *scrolls* on which to write.

- Long ago, s*cribes* used quill pens to hand-write the text in books. Books written in this manner often took years to complete.

- Johann Gutenberg, a German goldsmith, developed the printing press in the mid-15th century. His movable-type presses produced a decorative, textured type modeled after the Gothic handwriting of the period. His printing press revolutionized communication and allowed ideas to be shared with many people.

Pop-Out Posters

Young readers can create pop-out book posters to encourage others to read not only during National Children's Book Week, but throughout the entire year. Begin by asking students to create slogans promoting reading, then use the slogans to make the posters. Have each student fold a sheet of construction paper in half. Cut two slits perpendicular to the fold, about 2" in length and 2" apart, to form the top and bottom edges of a pop-out book. Unfold the paper and separate the cut section from the rest of the paper so that it makes a pop-out shaped like a book. Make two creases in the center of the pop-out book and attach a thin strip of paper to resemble a book spine. If a poster is displayed on a wall, attach tape to the top and bottom of the poster on the creased portion only. This will allow the book section to pop out. If desired, the poster can be folded slightly and made to stand on a flat surface.

READING

Borrow a Book

Encourage students to check out different books by borrowing them from classmates. Ask each child to bring a book from home, with permission, to use in a class book exchange. Keep a record of the books brought in and have each student place a bookmark with her name on it in his book. Let students keep a record of who read their books by completing the Book Exchange form (page 58) for each of their books. When a student wants to borrow the book, she can write her name and the date on the form. When the book is returned, the reader can write a thank you note to the lender.

Character Day

Create a class full of characters! Choose a day during Children's Book Week in which each child can dress like his favorite book character. Throughout the day, have classmates ask each character questions and try to guess the name and book in which he is featured. Set aside time for dressed-up students to read aloud portions of their books to the class, encouraging others to read the story.

Reading Super Star Bookmarks

Get students motivated about reading with a class reading challenge. Have the class set a goal to read a specific number of books. Chart the children's progress and when the goal is met, copy the reading super star bookmark (page 59) onto white poster board for each child as a reward. Let students color and cut out the bookmarks. If desired, use a craft knife to cut around the bottom half of the star, and then show students how to place the bookmark so the star slips over the book page.

Reading Buttons

Encourage students to *read, read, read*—especially during Children's Book Week—using student-designed buttons. To make a button, have students cut 3" circles from poster board and decorate them with slogans and artwork that promote reading. Punch a hole in each student's button for each book he has read during book week. Lace the holes with pieces of ribbon or yarn. Glue safety pins to the backs of the buttons for students to wear on their shirts.

Reading is Fun!

Reading Super Star!

Hunting for a Good Book

Send students on a treasure hunt for books! Choose a book and write clues about the characters, plot, and setting, as well as the location of the next clue, on copies of the book pattern (page 58). Students can use the clues to determine the title of the book. Begin the treasure hunt by placing the first clue in a location where students will see it easily and then hide the rest. The clues will lead students to the book. Each clue should be left for the next child to find. Tuck a note inside the book instructing students to see you for a prize. Reward students who find the book with a bookmark or 15 minutes of free reading time.

Clue #1: The story takes place on a rainy day.

Clue #2: A cat is the main character.

Clue #3: The story has rhyming words.

Answer: The Cat in the Hat.

Book Talk

Make books a hot topic in your classroom by organizing student book talks. Explain that many libraries and book stores hold book talks where groups discuss a book they have all read. Ask the class to brainstorm a list of books they would like to read and let each child pick a book from the list. Be sure that at least two people sign up to read any given book. Choose a date when students must have their books read and give out copies of the Book Talk worksheet (page 58) for students to complete. Pick a day and time for groups to talk about the book and complete the information on their worksheets. Combine the worksheets for each title and post them for prospective readers to see.

Reading Partners

By reading with enthusiasm, your students can help beginning readers share in the excitement of reading. Provide books that are suitable for younger students, such as *Green Eggs and Ham* by Dr. Seuss or *The Very Hungry Caterpillar* by Eric Carle. After students are familiar with the text, allow them to read the books aloud with expression, character voices, and excitement. Then, pair your students with younger children from other classes and have them read the books aloud to their partners during story time.

WRITING

Author's Journal

Sometimes the hardest part of writing is thinking of something to write about. Introduce students to a technique used by many authors—keeping a writing journal. Encourage students to jot down descriptions of people, surroundings, and other observations. When it's time to write, students can use their journal ideas as starting points.

Ideas

Characters

Planning a Story

Budding authors can organize their stories using the Map Your Story worksheet (page 57). Explain that an important part of writing is planning and organizing thoughts and ideas. Before students begin writing their stories, have them pre-write by completing the worksheet and deciding important details such as settings, main characters, problems, and solutions.

Drafting a Story

Once students have decided what to write about, they can begin first drafts of their stories. Have students use their completed Map Your Story worksheets (page 57) when writing the stories. Instruct your young writers to use descriptive words when writing about the setting and characters and use action words when describing what the characters are doing. Post lists of suggested words or phrases children can use in their stories, such as descriptive words, action words, sentence starters, etc. When the stories have been completed, students should check their own work for spelling, punctuation, and grammar.

It was a dark and stormy night...

Editor for a Day ✓

Encourage students to edit and proofread their classmates' work created in the *Drafting a Story* activity (above) by setting up an editing center. Place two large folders at the center and label one *To Proofread* and the other *Return to Writer*. Instruct students to attach the Proof-reader's Checklist (page 58) to their stories and place them in the *To Proofread* folder, then take out other students' papers to check. Each child should complete the checklist, then place the draft with the checklist into the *Return to Writer* folder to give to the writer for revisions. After revisions have been completed, collect the stories and review your young editors' proofreading skills.

*Fun activity!
—Editor*

Descriptive Words		Action Words	
bright	noisy	skipped	ran
funny	kind	jumped	whispered
beautiful	sweet	shouted	yelled

Sentence Starters

One day	First	Next
Then	Finally	At last

Proofreader's Checklist

Title _____ Writer _____

I have checked the story for: ☐ spelling ☐ punctuation

Some ideas for the story: _____

Proofreader _____

49

PUBLISHING

Publishing a Story

After the drafts and revisions have been completed in *Drafting a Story* and *Editor for a Day* activities (page 49), students will be ready to make a *dummy*. A dummy is a model of a book showing what writing and illustrations will go on each page. Children can write in the sentences and sketch out what will be drawn on the pages before putting the story into the actual book. To make a dummy, draw a box or space for each page on a large sheet of paper and decide how much writing and artwork will fit in the spaces. When a dummy has been completed, students will be ready to publish stories in a book format. Included here are several different types of books children can make to showcase their finished stories.

About the Author

After your young authors have completed their books, give them a moment in the spotlight with an *About the Author* bulletin board display. Have students interview and write about each other. Interviewers can ask about the author's families, favorite things, hobbies, and other books they have written. Interviewers can also take instant photographs which can be displayed on the bulletin board along with the informative paragraphs. If desired, students can also include *About the Author* pages in their finished books.

The Sea Urchin and the Rainbow Fish

Window-Blind Book

Fold-up books similar to the book described here originated in Asia, where people wanted to create books that could easily have pages added to them. When new pages were added, a long folded piece was glued to the bottom of the book.

Step 1   Fold a white sheet of 8½" x 11" paper in half.

Step 2   Fold the top section back over to the folded edge.

Step 3   Turn the paper over and fold the bottom section back over to the folded edge, creating an accordion-folded paper with four equal sections.

Step 4   With the paper still folded, punch a hole at each end, centered about ½" from the edge of the paper.

Step 5   Thread a length of yarn through the holes and tie at the top to close the book. To add pages, glue additional folded sheets of paper to the bottom of the book.

the Rainbow Fish

Pull-out Book

Pull-out books can incorporate a large piece of artwork that fills several pages. The amount of writing space on each page will depend on how many times the paper is folded.

Step 1 Accordion-fold a piece of a 11" x 17" white paper.

Step 2 Fold a sheet of 9" x 12" construction paper in half. Glue the back panel of the folded white paper to the inner folded side of the construction paper to make a book and cover.

Step 3 Cut a small piece of paper for a tab and label it *Pull*. Glue the paper tab underneath the edge of the top panel (see illustration) so the book pages can be opened by the reader.

The Best Clubhouse

Pull

GLUE

Shaped Book with Moveable Character

Character books can help students write different adventures from a single character's point of view. Choose a simple shape for the book and let each child choose a character whose story she will tell. For example, a house and child, school and student, or fire house and Dalmatian. To create a barn book, use the instructions below and the barn and chick patterns (page 59).

Step 1 Trace and cut out the barn pattern to create a front cover, back cover, and the desired number of book pages. Staple the pages between the covers to create a book.

Step 2 Cut out the chick pattern. Illustrate a scene on each page, leaving space for the chick.

Step 3 On the last page, cut out and glue a paper pocket for the chick. Tape a length of yarn to the back of the book. Tape the other end of the yarn to the back of the chick. Tuck the chick into the pocket.

Step 4 As you read the story, move the chick from page to page. At the end of the story, put the chick back in the pocket.

Shape Books

Shape books spark creativity. Have students choose a shape or simple outline to cut out on every page of these books, then design the text and artwork around them.

Step 1 Have students cut white paper to the desired size and staple the pages together into a book.

Step 2 Draw a shape or simple design on the top page. Help students cut out the design using a craft knife. Be sure to cut through all the pages.

Step 3 Write the text on the pages and then incorporate the shape into the artwork.

Step-by-Step Book

Encourage students to get their writing ideas in order by making step books. Use ordinal numbers to label the bottoms of each page to show how the steps progress.

Step 1 Stack 3 sheets of 8½" x 11" white paper so there is approximately 1" showing at the bottom of each page.

Step 2 Fold the stacked pages to create six overlapping sections. Staple near the fold.

Step 3 Write parts of the story under each overlapping flap of the book.

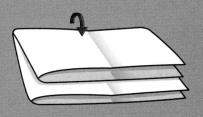

A Book from One Paper

This handy book idea uses one sheet of paper and is easy to fold.

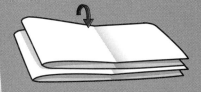

Step 1 Fold one sheet of 11" x 17" white paper in half vertically two times.

Step 2 Unfold the paper once and fold it in half horizontally.

Step 3 Open the paper and cut a slit on the center fold as shown.

Step 4 Refold the paper horizontally.

Step 5 Fold in half to make a 4-page book.

Pop-Up Books

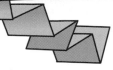

Add some fun to classroom stories with pop-up pages. Use the following ideas to create a pop-up book with variety or choose one technique and repeat it throughout a book.

Pop-Up Book Supplies
2 sheets of 8½" x 11" paper, cut in half
Scissors
Glue
Scrap paper

Accordion Pop-Ups

Step 1   Cut a strip of paper 5" long and 1" wide. Accordion-fold the strip of paper.

Step 2   Draw and cut out a character or object to glue to one end of the strip.

Step 3   Draw a scene on the page. Glue the other end of the folded strip to the page. Glue a piece of paper to the back of the page to reinforce the pop-up piece. When the page is opened, the character or object will jump from the page.

Book within a Book

Step 1   Use scrap paper to cut several 2½" x 2" rectangles. Stack the rectangles and fold along the middle.

Step 2   Draw a picture on each page.

Step 3   Glue the miniature book inside the larger book by putting a thin line of glue on the folded crease of the large book page. Place one of the folded miniature pages on the glue. Hold until the glue sets. Glue all of the miniature pages in this manner, one on top of the other, to make a little book within a big book.

Pop-up Tabs

Step 1   Fold one of the half sheets of paper in half. Draw 2 straight lines from the fold to the halfway point of the paper. Cut along these lines.

Step 2   Open the paper and gently push the tab out in the opposite direction of the fold.

Step 3   Refold the crease on the tab so it stands up.

Step 4   Pictures can be drawn on or glued to the cut-out. Glue another sheet of paper to the back of the page so the space behind the cut-out is not visible.

Parts that Move

Step 1   Draw a character, leaving space for a moveable piece to be added. (For instance, a dog with a movable tail.)

Step 2   Cut a strip of paper sized to match the character. Finish drawing the character on the strip of paper.

Step 3   Punch a hole on the piece and attach it to the character using a paper fastener. Glue another piece of paper to the back of the book page to hide the paper fastener.

53

Two Books in One

Every story has two sides, so have your students write about both in one book. Using a two-sided book, students can present two versions of the same story and gain an understanding of points of view.

Step 1   Accordion-fold a 6" x 18" strip of construction paper into three sections.

Step 2   Cut two sheets of 8¹/₂" x 11" white paper in half to make four 8¹/₂" x 5¹/₂" pieces. Fold these pieces in half.

Step 3   Open one flap of the folded construction paper. Match the creases of two folded white sheets of paper to the crease on the construction paper. Place paper clips over the edges of the papers to hold them in place. Use a thumbtack to make two small holes through all of the layers.

Step 4   Thread a length of yarn on an embroidery needle. Do not knot the end of the yarn. From the back of the construction paper, push the needle up through one of the holes. Then, push the needle down through the other hole, so both yarn ends are on the construction paper side.

Step 5   Even out the ends of the yarn and tie in a bow to secure the pages into the book. Turn the book over and repeat the steps on the other folded section of construction paper using the remaining sheets of white paper.

Flip Book

Allow students to focus on descriptive writing with silly results. Children can write their own phrases to make individual books or collaborate with classmates to create a class book.

Step 1   Fold several white, 8¹/₂" x 11" sheets of paper vertically into thirds.

Step 2   Then, fold the papers in half.

Step 3   Open the paper and turn it vertically. On the right side of the center fold, write a description of a character in the top section, an action phrase in the middle section, and a description of a setting in the bottom section.

Step 4   On the left side of the center fold, illustrate the character. Draw the head in the top section, the torso in the middle section, and the legs in the bottom section.

Step 5   Combine the pages and staple them between two sheets of construction paper. Cut along the three vertical folds on each page to separate them into three sections. Flip the pages of the book to create funny characters and scenes.

54

The furry little cat

curled up in a cozy cave

in the deep blue sea.

Stitch a Book

Students can create sewn bindings for their books just as many printers do. The finished binding can be covered with colored electrical tape or left uncovered so the stitching is visible.

Step 1   Provide two pieces of 5¹/₂" x 8¹/₂" poster board for each child. Use a pencil to mark small dots along the long edge of one of the poster board pieces. The dots should be ¹/₂" from the edge and about 1" apart.

Step 2   Place several pieces of 5¹/₂" x 8¹/₂" white paper between the two pieces of poster board, with the marked board on top. Place paper clips along the sides of the stack to keep the papers in place.

Step 3   Use a push pin to poke holes through the drawn dots. Be sure the pin goes through all the layers of paper.

Step 4   Thread an embroidery needle and knot the end. Poke the needle up through the bottom of the stack, then around and up through the bottom of the next hole. Continue whip-stitching to the end.

Step 5   Stitch the binding in the opposite direction to create a zigzag pattern.

Step 6   Knot the ends together, cut them, and hide the ends by tucking them behind the stitches.

Stick Bindings

Stick and rubber band bindings add a nice finishing touch to nature and science theme books. Any kind of stick can be used—twigs and dowels work especially well.

My Science Book
by Nathan

Step 1   Cut two book covers from poster board or heavy paper. Make the inside pages by cutting several sheets of white paper the same size as the book covers. Stack all the pages between the book covers with the marked cover on top. Use paper clips to hold the stacked papers together.

Step 2   Use a ruler and pencil to measure and mark two holes 1" from the edge in the top- and bottom-left corners of the cover. Poke a push pin through each hole.

Step 3   Enlarge the holes by sliding a pencil through them. Thread one end of a rubber band up from the bottom of the stack and place the stick or dowel (slightly longer than the cover) through the rubber band loop.

Step 4   Thread the opposite end of the rubber band through the other hole. Place the other end of the stick or dowel through this rubber band loop. Adjust the stick or dowel to the desired position.

55

MAKING BOOK COVERS

Marbleized Paper

Create eye-catching book covers with marbleized paper.

Step 1 Fill one large baking dish 2" deep with liquid starch. Fill another dish with cool water. Pour some acrylic paint into several paper cups and mix with water. Water down the paint until it slowly drips from a paintbrush. Drip the paints on the surface of the starch to create designs.

Starch

Step 2 When the surface has been covered with paint, run a feather, toothpick, or fork across the surface to make intricate designs, if desired.

Water

Step 3 Hold a piece of paper by opposite ends and gently lay it on the surface of the liquid starch. Do not let the paper sink under the surface. Hold the paper up and let the excess paint drip off for several seconds.

Step 4 Submerge the paper in the dish of water. Remove and hold up for several seconds allowing the excess water to drip away.

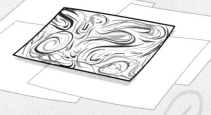

Step 5 Cover a flat surface with paper towels. Lay the paper (painted side up) on the towels to dry.

Fancy Printing

Students can make book cover designs and decorative letters using this printing technique.

Step 1 Cut a few clean foam meat trays into 2" x 2" sqares.

Step 2 Draw a large letter or simple design on a foam piece. If you are printing a letter, draw it backwards on the foam square so it will appear correctly when printed.

Step 3 Use a dull pencil to push down the foam surrounding the letter or design so that the letter or design is raised above the surface of the rest of the foam.

Step 4 With a paintbrush, apply acrylic paint to the raised portion.

Step 5 Gently push the foam square onto paper to create a print.

Name _____

Map Your Story

Title _____

① **Setting**	② **Characters**
Descriptive words:	**Descriptive words:**
③ **The story begins . . .**	④ **The problem is . . .**
⑤ **The problem is solved . . .**	⑥ **The story ends . . .**

Book Exchange

Title:									
Belongs to:									
Name:		Date:							

book

Book Talk

Name _____ Book Title_____

Author_____

Did you like the book? Why or why not?_____

_____

_____

Write about a character you liked and tell why._____

_____

_____

Proofreader's Checklist

Title _____ Writer_____

I have checked the story for: ☐ spelling ☐ punctuation

Some ideas for the story: _____

_____

_____

Proofreader _____ Date_____

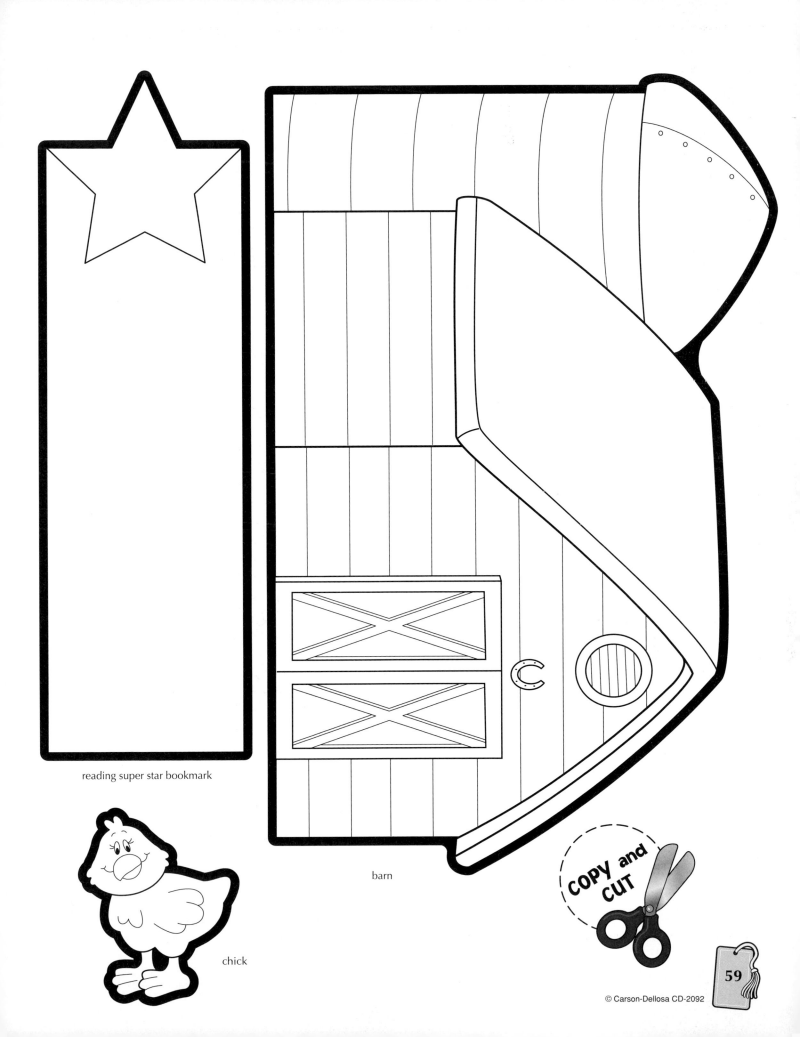

reading super star bookmark

barn

chick

COPY and CUT

59

Hello Across the World

Bonjour, Guten Tag, Jambo, and Shalom!
In other words, Hello! World Hello Day, celebrated
each year on November 21, provides a fun opportunity
for your class to learn the value of a simple greeting. You
can celebrate this unique event in your classroom, in your school,
or expand your students' horizons and say "hello"
across the world! Let your students enjoy expressing
peace and goodwill.

Did You Know?

Anyone can participate in World Hello Day and promote peace in the world by simply greeting ten people. The event, started in 1973, has been observed by people in 180 countries.

To say "hello" to everyone in the world, you would have to learn at least 2,796 languages and say *hello* 5,720,000,000 times!

Literature Selections

Children from Australia to Zimbabwe by Maya Ajmera & Anna Rhesa Versola: Charlesbridge Publishing, 1997. (Informational picture book, 64 pg.) Provides an A-Z profile of 25 countries and the imaginary Xanadu.

Children Just Like Me by Barnabas & Anabel Kindersley: DK Publishing, 1995. (Informational picture book, 82 pg.) The author and photographer traveled to 31 countries to provide a personal look at children's lives.

World Hello Day web site address: http://www.worldhelloday.org

Say Hello to the World!

Help your students become fluent in *Hello!* Create a display noting ways to say hello in other languages. Let each student familiarize himself with the different greetings and choose a favorite. Cover the display and let children take turns standing in front of the class and saying "hello" in their preferred way. Let students guess which language is being spoken.

Language	Meaning	Greeting	Pronunciation
• Arabic	good day	Al Salaam a'alaykum	(ahl sah•LAHM ah ah•LAY•koom)
• Chinese	hello	Ni hao	(nee HaOW)
• French	good day	Bonjour	(bohn•ZHOOR)
• German	good day	Guten tag	(GOOT•en tahk)
• Hawaiian	hello	Aloha	(ah•LOH•hah)
• Hebrew	peace	Shalom	(sha•LOHM)
• Italian	good day	Buon giorno	(bwohn JOR•noh)
• Japanese	good day	Konichiwa	(koh•NEE•chee•wah)
• Spanish	hello	Hola	(OH•lah)
• Swahili	hello	Jambo	(JAM•bo)
• American Sign Language	Touch temple with right hand and move hand away from forehead (similar to a salute).		

Greetings Around the World

Greeting others is always a sign of good manners—but the methods vary in different countries. Encourage children to think about any unspoken rules for greetings in the United States. Ask them if they greet adults in the same way they greet their friends and if they use any gestures in their greetings, such as waving, shaking hands, nodding their heads, etc. Inform students that in Japan, children bow from the waist as a form of greeting. French children greet close friends and family with a kiss on each cheek, while Korean children bow and nod their heads. Let children practice good greeting manners in multicultural ways!

All in Favor of Peace, Trace Your Hand!

Dove-in-Hand Wreaths will help students remember the purpose of World Hello Day. Let each student trace his hand onto different colors of construction paper, cut out the shapes, and then overlap and glue them onto a doughnut shape cut from poster board. Children can cut dove shapes out of white paper or felt to add to the wreath. Have children write *peace* on their doves in several different languages.

Maria McCarson
4321 Parkmont Way
Bluesboro, PA 10001

Dafna Schwartz
Herzl St.
Haifa, Israel

Dear Dafna,
Thank you for telling me about your life in Israel. Math is also my favorite subject! Did you learn to speak English at school or home? I only know one word in Hebrew—Shalom. I've tasted felafel before but I've never even heard of burekas. What are they? Write soon!

Your pen pal,
Maria

Hello Out There!

Students can say "hello" to children across the world and learn about other cultures by writing to pen pals. Obtain addresses from pen pal organizations (these can be found on the Internet) or sources within your school system. Give students a list of basic information to include in their letters and let them question pen pals about where they live, what they like to do, etc.

Hello Hello Hello Hello Hello Hello

The Ripple Effect

Students can use math skills to find out that sharing a simple greeting can have big results. Ask students to calculate how many people could be affected by their greetings on World Hello Day. If one person says "hello" to ten people, who each say "hello" to ten more people, how many people have been greeted?

61

VETERANS DAY

Veterans Day is celebrated in the United States on November 11th. It is a day to honor all veterans of the armed forces by showing respect and thanks for their service to their country. Celebrating Veterans Day is the perfect opportunity to give students a sense of history and patriotism.

Did You Know?

☆ A veteran is someone who has served in the armed forces. The armed forces of the United States include the Army, the Air Force, the Navy, the Marines, and the Coast Guard.

☆ Veterans Day was originally known as Armistice Day and was declared a national holiday in 1938. The Armistice was the agreement that ended World War I in 1918—the fighting stopped on the eleventh hour of the eleventh day of the eleventh month. The name of the holiday was changed to Veterans Day in 1954.

☆ Many cities and communities observe a moment of silence, beginning at 11:00 a.m. Some cities also hold parades on this holiday.

Literature Selections

Veterans Day by Mir Tamim Ansary: Heinemann Library, 1999. (Informational book, 32 pg.) Provides a brief history of Veterans Day with many color photographs; includes a glossary and a list of important dates.

In Flanders Fields: The Story of the Poem by John McCrae by Linda Granfield: Doubleday, 1996. (Informational book, 32 pg.) Contains John McCrae's poem in its entirety, juxtaposed with beautiful, impressionistic illustrations; background material on the era; and reproductions of period postcards and photographs.

Why Poppies?

Teach why poppies are associated with Veterans Day and let students make paper ones to wear and share. In World War I, a battle was fought in a part of Europe called Flanders. Soldiers lost in the battle were buried in a field of red poppies which became known as Flanders Field. Red poppies are worn on Veterans Day in honor of the soldiers who fought at Flanders. You will need 6" lengths of green pipe cleaners and 5" squares of red and yellow tissue paper. Layer 4-6 squares of red tissue paper, then top with 1-2 squares of yellow tissue paper, lining up the edges. Accordion-fold the tissue paper squares. Twist one end of the pipe cleaner around the middle of the folded tissue to secure. Separate the layers of tissue paper by pulling each layer toward the center to create the flower shape. To wear their poppies, students can tuck the pipe cleaner "stems" into a buttonhole on their clothing or use safety pins to attach them.

Reward Yourself!

Have students create their own award medals to commemorate Veterans Day. The Armed Forces of the United States give out awards to honor distinguished heroism in war. The Medal of Honor is the highest decoration for gallantry in the United States and the oldest official American medal still awarded. (See encyclopedias for color photos of other types of medals.)

- Mix 4 cups flour, 1 cup salt, and 1½ cups water together to form a dough. Knead the dough for 10 minutes. Divide the dough in half. To prevent drying, keep the reserved portion covered with plastic wrap until ready to use.

- Roll the dough to a ¼" thickness, then cut shapes using heart, circle, or star cookie cutters dipped in flour. (If dough breaks, use water to join the pieces of dough together.)

- Place the shapes on cookie sheets, and make a hole at the top of each with a drinking straw. Designs can be pressed halfway into the dough using small star- or heart-shaped objects.

- Bake at 300° for approximately 1-1½ hours. Cool the shapes on wire racks or foil.

Have students paint the medals with gold, silver, bronze, or purple acrylic craft paint. Thread a ribbon through the hole at the top of each shape and tie the ends to form a "necklace" that each student can wear. (The medals can be preserved by coating them with polyurethane or spray acrylic once they are decorated.)

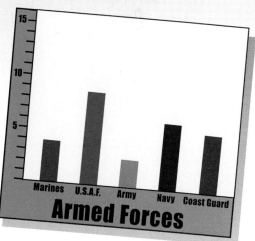

Visit a Veteran!

Take students to a nearby veterans' hospital or facility. Call the Veterans Administration to find the location nearest you. Contact the facility to arrange a visit and ask if students can perform a special program. Students can plan a performance of skits, patriotic songs, poem recitations, etc. Allow time for students to visit with the veterans. Students may also want to make paper poppies to share (*Why Poppies?*, page 62) or deliver handwritten letters expressing their gratitude for the veterans' service.

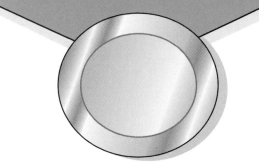

A Math Veteran

Celebrate the day with veteran-inspired math by creating a graph of the class's favorite branches of service. Label one axis of the graph with the different branches of the armed forces. Let each student "vote" for their favorite branch. Play the "theme song" of the winning branch, if desired.

Armed Forces graph:
Marines | U.S.A.F. | Army | Navy | Coast Guard
Armed Forces

Anchors Aweigh—Navy
Off We Go Into the Wild Blue Yonder—Air Force
The Army Goes Rolling Along—Army
From the Halls of Montezuma—Marines
Always Ready—Coast Guard

63

Gobbling Good Thanksgiving Fun

Your students will gobble up these Thanksgiving craft, snack, and game ideas! After adorning your classroom with festive turkey decorations, invite students to enjoy a Thanksgiving treat complete with student-made table favors. Remind students to be thankful for what they have as they enjoy preparing for Thanksgiving.

Did You Know?

The turkey may have gotten its name because of the *turc, turc, turc* sound it makes when it is frightened.

The wild turkey is native to both North and South America.

Literature Selections

A Turkey for Thanksgiving by Eve Bunting: Clarion Books, 1995. (Picture Book, 32 pg.) When Mr. and Mrs. Moose invite a turkey to Thanksgiving, everyone is in for a big surprise.

Thanksgiving Day by Gail Gibbons: Holiday House, 1985. (Picture book, 32 pg.) Explains the history and customs of Thanksgiving and how people celebrate the holiday today.

Cranberry Thanksgiving by Wende and Harry Devlin: Aladdin Books, 1990. (Picture book, 38 pg.) A special guest is invited to Thanksgiving dinner with Maggie and her grandmother. Grandmother makes her secret recipe cranberry bread for her guests.

Gobble Game

Students can feast on candy corn while having tons of fun playing this Thanksgiving game. Let students use the gobble game grid and game pieces (page 71) to make game boards. Have students choose nine picture pieces to color, cut out, and glue to their grids in any order. Give each student a handful of candy corn to use as markers. Cut out a set of all the game pieces and place them in a container. To play the game, select a game piece from the container, call out the name, and have students cover the picture with candy corn if it appears on their game boards. The player or players who cover a row of three pictures across, down, or diagonally wins. After the game, let students enjoy the candy corn as a treat.

Tubular Turkeys

These colorful decorations will brighten up any turkey day. Give each child a short cardboard tube and have him cut slits approximately 2" long and 1/2" wide around one end of the tube. To make feet for the turkey, cut two of the slits slightly longer and leave a 1" space in between. Cut points at the bottom of these two pieces to resemble turkey feet. Push the remaining cardboard pieces forward. Copy the turkey body pattern (page 70) onto brown paper and cut out. Apply glue to the uncut end of the tube and attach the turkey body pattern. Color the base of the tube brown and color the cardboard pieces to resemble turkey feathers.

Turkey Fans

Turn a simple paper fan into a unique Thanksgiving decoration.

1. Hold a 12" x 18" sheet of white or yellow construction paper vertically. Accordion-fold the paper from top to bottom in 2" sections.

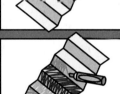

2. Open up the paper and color each section red, gold, yellow, brown, or tan.

3. Staple the pleated paper in the center, then fold the paper in half and glue the folds together, creating a large fan.

4. Cut a 4" circle from yellow paper and glue it to the center of the fan. Cut a 2" circle from brown paper and glue it in the center of the larger circle. Use scrap paper for the eyes, beak, and wattle and glue them on the small circle to make a turkey face. Secure the folded area together with a staple.

Turkey in the Clay

Grab some clay and let your students roll out an unusual turkey decoration. Give each child 12 wooden craft sticks and one half of a craft stick. Use markers to color the sticks red, orange, yellow, and brown. Give each student a piece of self-hardening clay and have her roll the clay into a small ball. Push the 12 craft sticks into the clay ball and position them so they resemble turkey feathers. Push the craft stick half in front of the feathers. Draw and cut out a turkey face and glue it to the half craft stick. After the clay has dried, paint it brown.

Tissue Paper Turkey Wreaths

Add a touch of Thanksgiving to your classroom with these turkey wreaths. Give each student a paper plate and instruct him to cut out the center. Provide 1" squares of colored tissue paper. Spread a thin layer of glue around the rim of the plate. Attach the tissue paper squares using the end of a pencil. When the tissue paper has dried, cut a turkey face from brown paper and add eyes, a beak, and a wattle. Glue the bottom of the turkey face to the inside edge of the paper plate. Cut out two turkey feet from colorful paper and glue them to the outside edge of the plate. Punch a hole at the top of the plate, thread a length of yarn through, and knot the ends to create a hanger.

Thanksgiving Greetings

These pop-up turkeys are just right for sending holiday greetings.
1. Copy a class supply of the turkey greeting card pattern (page 72) on heavy paper.
2. Instruct students to color the turkeys, then fold the paper on the dotted line with the picture inside.
3. Unfold and cut the heavy pattern outline above the fold, leaving the surrounding paper intact.
4. Stand the card up, refold on the dotted line, and crease the cut-out feathers forward so they pop up.
5. Have students write Thanksgiving greetings on the fronts of the cards.

HAPPY THANKSGIVING

red
yellow

A Cup Full of Turkey Fun

Fill your classroom with turkey time fun! Give each student a small paper or plastic cup, then wrap and tape a piece of brown tissue paper around the outside. For the feathers, draw a simple scalloped design in three sizes (see illustration) and have students trace and cut out the feathers from three colors of construction paper. Turn the cup over and glue the feathers on one side. Complete the decoration by drawing and cutting out a turkey face to glue on the front.

Turkey Treats

These Thanksgiving turkeys are stuffed with candies and treats for your students. To make a turkey, give each child a short cardboard tube and a piece of brown tissue paper that is long enough to extend over the ends of the tube. Wrap the paper around the tube and secure it with clear tape. Twist the paper closed on one end of the tube only. Tie a length of yarn around the twisted paper to keep it closed. Place small candies or other treats inside the tube, then twist, tape, and tie the other end closed. Give students copies of the turkey feather pattern (page 70) to trace onto construction paper. Cut out the feathers and glue them to one side of the tube. Crumple a small piece of tissue paper and glue it to the top of the tube for the turkey's head. Use markers to add eyes, a beak, and a wattle to the turkey treat holder.

Mini Pumpkin Pies

Students will enjoy making and eating miniature pumpkin pies in tartlet crusts!

16 unbaked tartlet shells
3/4 cup sugar
1/2 teaspoon salt
1 teaspoon ground cinnamon
1/2 teaspoon ground ginger
1/4 teaspoon ground cloves
2 eggs
1 15-ounce can pumpkin
1 12-ounce can evaporated milk

Preheat oven to 425°. Mix sugar, salt, cinnamon, ginger, and cloves together. In a separate bowl, lightly beat eggs. Stir in pumpkin and the mixed dry ingredients. Gradually stir in evaporated milk. Fill each tartlet about 3/4 full with pie filling. Bake for 15 minutes. Reduce temperature to 350° and continue baking for 40-50 minutes or until a knife inserted into the center of a tartlet comes out clean. Cool before serving. Top with whipped cream or ice cream, if desired. Makes 16 tartlets. Let students solve the secret code game (page 70) while they enjoy the pumpkin pies.

Where Do I Sit?

These turkey place cards will help each student find his seat at the Thanksgiving table. For each child, cut a 6" x 5" piece of poster board. Hold the poster board vertically and draw a line across each side, approximately 2" from the edges. Fold the poster board on these lines and stand it upright on the work surface. Give each child a piece of 5" x 7" construction paper. Have him accordion-fold the paper vertically. Fold the pleated paper in half and glue the edges together to form a fan. Glue the bottom of the fan on the flat top of the folded poster board. Have students cut out and color a turkey face and copies of the turkey wing patterns (page 70). Glue the wings to the left and right edges of the poster board, and glue the face onto the front. Personalize the place cards by having students write their names on the fronts. Save seats at your Thanksgiving table with the place cards or allow students to use them at their desks, the lunchroom, or at home for Thanksgiving Day.

A Meal Fit for a Turkey

Let students gobble up their Thanksgiving feasts on handmade place mats. Begin by having each student collect eight brightly colored fall leaves. Give each child a poster board rectangle and have him arrange the leaves to resemble the feathers on a turkey. Glue the leaves in place after using markers to draw a turkey body, feet, and other details. When the designs are complete, cover each place mat with clear self-adhesive paper or laminate. Use the place mats to add a festive touch to any Thanksgiving feast.

Thanksgiving Table Favors

Children can enjoy making these festive table favors and sharing them at home. Give each student a small paper or plastic cup and a copy of the turkey body and turkey feather patterns (page 70). Have students color and cut out the patterns. Glue the body pattern to the front of the cup and the feathers to the back.

Ring Around the Turkey

Students can make holiday napkin rings to take home and share with their families on Thanksgiving Day. Cut long cardboard tubes into 2" sections. Give each student enough cardboard sections for all of her family members and have her color the outsides using markers. Copy a class supply of the turkey napkin ring pattern (page 70) for students to color and cut out. Glue the turkey pattern to the side of the cardboard section to finish the napkin ring. Fold and place a holiday napkin in each ring.

Turkeys Galore Tablecloth

Your students will be seeing turkeys everywhere when they enjoy a Thanksgiving meal at this holiday table. Use handprints to make a decorative tablecloth by having students paint their hands with brown paint. Instruct students to press their painted hands onto a large sheet of white butcher paper. When the prints have dried, provide markers for students to use to add details to the turkeys. Use the tablecloth to cover a large table, then invite students to enjoy a Thanksgiving treat, such as *Mini Pumpkin Pies* (page 67).

Name _____

Use the secret code to answer the riddle.

What kind of key will not open a door?

A ___ ___ ___ ___ ___ ___

SECRET CODE

K =   E =   R =   T =   Y =   U =

secret code game

turkey wings

COPY and CUT

turkey body   turkey feather   turkey napkin ring

GOBBLE

cornucopia	log cabin	turkey	corn
apple	leaves	pilgrim cap	acorn
pie	haystack	wheat	pumpkin

© Carson-Dellosa CD-2092

gobble game grid and game pieces

71

turkey greeting card

COPY and CUT

72

The Pilgrims, the Wampanoag, and the First Thanksgiving

The Pilgrims

On September 6, 1620, 102 passengers set sail on the *Mayflower*. These Pilgrims were a group of men, women, and children who left England to settle in America. Some were Separatists who wanted freedom to worship in their own way. Others hoped to make better lives for themselves. Originally bound for Virginia, the 66-day voyage ended near Cape Cod, Massachusetts on November 11, 1620. The Pilgrims settled in Plymouth because of its fields, streams, and safe harbor. Only 51 Pilgrims survived the first winter due to sickness and lack of food. Despite the hardships, no pilgrm returned to England when the captain and surviving crew of the *Mayflower* returned to England on April 5, 1621. The Pilgrims learned agricultural skills from the native people and worked hard to survive. Eventually, other English ships brought more settlers and resources to Plymouth.

Did You Know?

- The Pilgrims planned to sail on two ships—the *Mayflower* and the *Speedwell*. Both ships left England on August 5, 1620, but had to return because the *Speedwell* was leaky. It could not be repaired, so passengers crowded on the *Mayflower*.

- The Pilgrims lived on the *Mayflower* throughout the first winter while they built their houses.

- A baby boy was born during the journey across the ocean. His parents named him Oceanus, in honor of the voyage.

Literature Selections

Across the Wide Dark Sea: The Mayflower Journey by Jean Van Leeuwen: Dial Books for Young Readers, 1995. (Picture book, 32 pg.) Tells of the famous voyage from the point of view of a pilgrim boy sailing to a new land with his family.

N.C. Wyeth's Pilgrims by Robert San Souci: Chronicle Books, 1991. (Picture book, 40 pg.) N.C. Wyeth's murals complement this history of pilgrim life.

Sarah Morton's Day: A Day in the Life of a Pilgrim Girl by Kate Waters: Scholastic Inc., 1989. (Picture book, 32 pg.) Photographs and a first person account of a day in the life of a pilgrim girl at the Plimoth (sic) Plantation living museum. *Samuel Eaton's Day* (40 pg.) and *On the Mayflower*, (40 pg.) by the same author, are presented in the same format and provide additional insight into pilgrim life.

The Pilgrims of Plimoth (sic) by Marcia Sewall: Simon & Schuster, 1986. (Picture book, 48 pg.) Colorful, full-page illustrations accompany text detailing the history and daily life of Plimoth Colony.

Traveling Trunks

The Pilgrims were the first passengers to sail on the *Mayflower*, which was built to be a cargo ship. Because of this, space was very limited for the Pilgrims and their belongings. Each family was given a large chest to fill with items they would need in their new homes. Many families took tools, cooking utensils, and clothing. Most items not necessary for survival were left behind. Have children make traveling trunks and think of personal items they would want to take with them. Copy the trunk pattern (page 83) on brown construction paper and the list pattern (page 83) on white paper for each student to cut out. On the list patterns, have students write the things they would take. Cut a small slit on the dotted line on each trunk pattern using a craft knife and slide the list through until only the word *Pull* is visible. Pull the tabs to find out what students would have taken.

Set Sail on the Mayflower

It is not known whether the *Mayflower* actually landed at Plymouth Rock, but it is remembered today as a symbol of the Pilgrims and their bravery and determination. Help the *Mayflower* sail to Plymouth Rock with this moveable ship craft. Trace the *Mayflower* pattern (page 83) on a sheet of paper folded in half, so that the bottom of the pattern is on the fold. Cut through both layers without cutting the folded edge. Color the ship and write facts about the *Mayflower* on each sail. Open the pattern and place a 24" length of yarn along the folded edge. Tape two craft sticks inside the pattern to help it stand upright, and glue the top and sides closed. Fold a 12" x 5" strip of blue construction paper in half lengthwise and cut a wavy line across the top to resemble waves. Cut a rock shape from paper, label it *Plymouth Rock*, and glue it to the left end of the strip. Cut a green circle from paper, label it *England,* and glue it to the right end of the strip. Place the ship inside the strip with the yarn extending out on both sides. Staple the ends of the strip closed. "Sail" the ship to Plymouth Rock by pulling the piece of yarn on the left side.

The Mayflower was a cargo ship.

The Mayflower didn't leak.

Pilgrims lived on the Mayflower while they built houses.

The Mayflower was made of wood.

Plymouth Rock

England

Rules to Live By

After the *Mayflower* landed in Plymouth, the Pilgrims realized they needed to work together in order to survive. The *Mayflower Compact* was the Pilgrims' promise to live by fair laws in the New World. The men who signed the *Mayflower Compact* agreed to stay together and follow any laws that were made. Have children brainstorm a classroom compact where students agree to treat each other fairly and follow classroom rules. Copy the classroom compact onto a large piece of chart paper and have each student sign it. Post the compact as a reminder to students to treat each other fairly.

Room 14 Compact
The students in Room 14 agree to listen to what our classmates have to say. When there is a problem or an argument, we will work it out by talking about it. We will follow the classroom rules and treat each other kindly. Signed,

John Shane Beth Ellie
Lisa Gati Atih Aldelfa
Carlos Andy Bruce

Pilgrim House

Pilgrim houses were constructed with clapboard siding and thatched roofs. Clapboards are plain planks of wood made from trees split vertically up the middle. Thatching is done by overlapping tied bundles of straw across the roof frame. Because the Pilgrims were not able to bring many items with them to America, they did not have the right tools for shaping stones for chimneys. Instead, they made their chimneys by weaving reeds (wattlework) through a wooden frame and covering the reeds and wood with clay. Create 3-dimensional pictures of pilgrim houses, using craft sticks as clapboards and miniwheat cereal as thatching. Make a chimney with toothpicks and cover it with clay. A pilgrim house would not be complete without a kitchen garden (a small vegetable and herb garden) near the house. Plot out the garden with toothpicks, then glue on green tissue paper herbs and vegetables. See page 18 for a bulletin board idea using the pilgrim houses.

Pilgrim Paper Doll

Pilgrims' clothing was actually colorful, not black and white, as traditionally portrayed. Men and women wore plain linen undershirts and stockings held up by garters and leather shoes (no buckles!). Men wore knee-length breeches, doublets (fitted jackets), and felt hats. Fancy collars and cuffs were added to dress up everyday outfits. Women wore several petticoats, ankle-length wool over-skirts, fitted waistcoats, long aprons, and coifs (linen caps). Children wore long gowns until the age of seven, when they changed to small versions of adult clothing. Give each child a copy of a pilgrim boy or girl pattern (page 84). Include copies of the dressed pilgrim boy and girl for reference. Have students color the dolls and then draw, color, cut out, and glue on the articles of clothing.

Recitation

There was not a school in Plymouth for many years, so if parents wanted their children to read and write, they had to teach them themselves. Children learned to read the Bible and were expected to memorize psalms and other passages and recite them. Give students a feel for what learning was like in Plymouth. Provide books of poetry and ask students to choose a poem to memorize. After a week of memorizing and practicing, let each child recite his poem for the class. Ask students how they can use memorization and recitation to help them in school.

75

Homemade Butter

A typical day for pilgrim children would include many chores, such as fetching water and firewood, and caring for animals and younger children. A chore done by many children was churning butter. Butter was made by skimming the cream from milk and stirring it in a butter churn until the butter fat separated in clumps from the rest of the cream. Let students make a small amount of butter to get an idea of what hard work churning butter must have been. Supply a thick jar, such as a canning jar, containing one cup of heavy whipping cream. Add a clean marble to the jar to act as the "churn." Let students take turns shaking the jar for about 15-20 minutes, until a lump of butter forms. Drain the liquid, mix in a pinch of salt, and spread on some bread to eat.

Nine Men's Morris

Pilgrim children sometimes played board games drawn on barrel tops. Play *Nine Men's Morris* using the board game design in the diagram below. Draw the board and copy one for each pair of students. Give each student nine game pieces (beans, buttons, etc.) The game is played by taking turns putting a game piece on places where lines meet. When a player gets three pieces in a vertical or horizontal line, he removes one of his opponent's pieces. When all pieces are played, continue the game by moving remaining pieces to adjacent line intersections. A player wins when her opponent has only two pieces left.

Diagram

Marbles

Marbles, or knickers, as they called them, was a popular game among pilgrim children. One marble game involved rolling marbles into a special box called a *knicker box*. A knicker box can be made from a shoe box. **1)** Cut the box top in half. **2)** Measure one half of the box top to be as tall as the shoe box. Cut off the excess. **3)** Draw and cut three arches along the bottom of the cut half and tape it to the other half at a right angle. Tuck the edges of the cut half inside the other half's edges. **4)** Put the lid back on so the arched part stands up in the middle. Let marbles roll across the top of the lid and bounce off the outside wall of the box. If the marble goes through one of the arches and does not bounce back out, the player earns a point. Take turns rolling the marbles and play until one player reaches ten points.

76

The Wampanoag

The *Wampanoag* (wampa•NO•og) are the Native people who lived in Massachusetts before the Pilgrims arrived. A Wampanoag leader is called a *sachem* (SAY•chum) and each of his councilmen is called a *pniese* (pa•NEES). When the Pilgrims arrived in Plymouth, the Wampanoag were living inland, away from the cold sea winds. During summer, they would move near the coast to plant corn and other crops. Hunting, fishing, and gathering were other ways to provide food. Traveling was done by foot or in a *mishoon* (mih•SHOON), a dugout canoe. The common clothing consisted of a breechclout (like an apron with a front and back), a mantle (worn over one shoulder), and moccasinash (plural of moccasin.) Their clothes were sewn from deer skin, and furs were often worn or used as blankets during the winter months. Today the Wampanoag still pass their traditions and customs from generation to generation.

Did You Know?

• Wampanoag means *Eastern People*, *People of the Dawn*, or *People of the First Light*.
• Many Wampanoag still live in Massachusetts and Rhode Island. Two of the best known groups live in Mashpee on Cape Cod and Gay Head on Martha's Vineyard.
• Corn, squash, and beans, staple foods of the Wampanoag, were not indigenous to the New England area. Corn and beans came from the southwest and Central America. Legend suggests that they were brought to the Wampanoag by a crow.

Literature Selections

Tapenum's Day: A Wampanoag Indian Boy in Pilgrim Times by Kate Waters: Scholastic Inc., 1996. (Picture book, 40 pg.) Photographs and a first person account of a day in the life of a Wampanoag Indian boy at the Hobbamock Homesite at the Plimoth (sic) Plantation living museum.

Clambake: A Wampanoag Tradition by Russel M. Peters: Lerner Publications Co., 1992. (Picture book, 48 pg.) A modern day Wampanoag boy learns from his grandfather about the tradition of preparing a clambake.

The Children of the Morning Light by Manitongquat: Simon & Schuster, 1994. (Storybook, 80 pg.) An elder and storyteller of the Assonet Wampanoag shares 11 traditional Wampanoag tales.

A Wampanoag House

A Wampanoag house, or *wetu* (WEE•too), was made by bending tree saplings into a dome and covering it with mats of woven cattail reeds or sheets of bark. A chimney was left in the top of the wetu, and an opening was left for a door, often covered with a mat that could be rolled up. Wampanoags built a fire in each wetu and placed mats inside for sleeping. Let each child create a wetu. Gather a square of cardboard, four pipe cleaners, modeling clay, rubber cement, and a paper bag for each child. Make bark rubbings on the bags with brown crayon to resemble sheets of bark, then follow the directions below. When the wetus are finished, put them together in a village, adding details such as a cornfield, shrubs, mats, etc.

1. Arrange six small balls of clay in a circle on the cardboard.
2. Press the end of a pipe cleaner into one clay ball. Press the other end into the clay ball opposite it. Repeat with two more pipe cleaners. Create a chimney by arranging the pipe cleaners to intersect in a triangular shape.
3. Cut the last pipe cleaner into four sections. Wrap sections around the intersecting corners of the triangular shape.
4. Wrap a pipe cleaner section between two pipe cleaners for a door.
5. Tear the paper bag into strips and use white glue to glue them to the pipe cleaners. Cover the wetu, leaving the chimney and door open.

A Wetu Mat

To complement the wetu houses, let students make mats to place in front of the doors or inside as sleeping mats. Cut a small square and several short strips from a paper bag. Fold the square in half and make parallel, 1" cuts through the fold, being careful not to cut all the way to the edge of the paper. Open the square and weave the small strips through the slits.

Clay Pots

The Wampanoag made pottery with clay dug from river banks. One common pottery technique was coiling. Make coiled pots from self-hardening clay. Roll the clay into long snakelike rolls. Coil the clay to make a circular base. Lay coils on top of each other around the outside of the base to build up the walls of the pot. Pinch the coils together and smooth out the sides. Before the pots dry, press patterns into the sides with pine cones or acorn tops as the Wampanoag may have done.

Gathering Basket

Wampanoag women not only wove the mats used to make wetus, but also wove gathering baskets. This type of weaving was called *twining* and involved interlacing fibers (called *weavers* or *wefts*) around rigid vertical fibers. A braided strap was often attached for carrying. To make a twined basket, use yarn for weavers and a small plastic cup for the rigid vertical fibers.

1. Cut narrow sections from the plastic cup, leaving thin vertical slats.
2. Pick two colors of yarn and cut into 18" lengths. Tie two pieces of the same color yarn together and slip over one of the plastic cup slats. Arrange the knot so it is inside the cup.
3. Weave the yarns in the same direction around the cup; alternate so that when one yarn goes over a slat, the other goes under.
4. Change colors by tying a new color of yarn to each of the old colors, arranging the knots so they are inside the basket.
5. Continue until the whole basket is woven. Knot the yarn ends on the inside to secure.
6. Cut three equal lengths of yarn and tie a knot in one end. Tape to a desk and braid the yarns. Tie a knot in the other end and then remove the tape.
7. Tie the braid to either side of the basket.

Snow Snakes

A game that many Wampanoag children played in winter was *Snow Snakes*. Children found a long stick in the woods and whittled it to look like a snake. Then, the stick was oiled and pushed down a track in the snow. The child whose stick went the farthest was the winner. To play indoor *Snow Snakes* with your class, roll out a length of white butcher paper. Tape one end of the paper to a table and the other end to the floor for a snow hill. Let each student cut out a snake shape from construction paper and tape it to the top of an unsharpened pencil. To race the "snakes," allow pairs of children to drop their snakes down the "snow hill." Let the winner of each race compete with the next player.

Wampanoag Hunting

The Wampanoag relied heavily on hunting for their food, especially during the winter. Hunting was done either by setting traps or with an *ahtomp* (ah•TOMP) and *kouhquodt* (COW•quat) (bow and arrow). Let students make a display of Wampanoag hunting tools. Have each student glue a straight stick to poster board or cardboard and draw on an arrowhead and glue long feathers (available at craft stores) to the ends of their arrows. Have students draw a bow and glue string to it. The quiver can be made from a construction paper tube. Ask students to label their arrows *kouhquodt*, the bows *ahtomp*, and the quiver *petan* (pee•TAN). Display the Wampanoag hunting posters on a bulletin board.

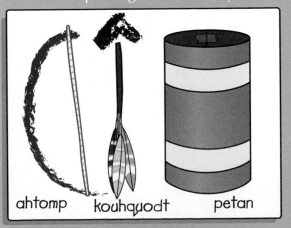

ahtomp   kouhquodt   petan

79

The First Thanksgiving

Contact between the Pilgrims and the Native People of New England began when Chief Samoset, visiting the Wampanoag from Maine, walked into the Plymouth settlement and said "Welcome" in English. Samoset had learned some English from fur traders near his village. He introduced the Pilgrims to Squanto, who taught the Pilgrims how to live and survive in New England. Samoset and Squanto also helped the Pilgrims and the Wampanoag negotiate a peace treaty. With the help of Samoset and Squanto, the Pilgrims had a plentiful harvest that fall and in October of 1621, the Pilgrims invited Massasoit, the Wampanoag sachem (chief) to a harvest celebration of thanksgiving. Massasoit came with 90 Wampanoag men and a large supply of deer meat to contribute to the feast. Along with the feasting they played games, danced to music, and demonstrated their skills with muskets and bows and arrows. The celebration lasted for three days.

Did You Know?

- Both the Wampanoag and Pilgrims had harvest celebrations of their own before the one they shared in 1621. The Wampanoag celebrated the Green Corn Ceremony (see page 31) when the corn was nearly ripe and the Pilgrims celebrated the Harvest Home in England with games and a feast.
- The Pilgrims did not celebrate Thanksgiving every year. Days of thanksgiving were declared at different times of the year for other reasons besides good harvests. Thanksgiving was not an annually celebrated national holiday until Abraham Lincoln declared it so in 1863.
- The foods eaten at the First Thanksgiving included turkey, venison, fish, clams, corn bread, and squash. Some things that we eat today at Thanksgiving were not eaten then, including potatoes (not grown in New England then), cranberry sauce (no sugar to sweeten the berries), and pumpkin pie (a pudding made with pumpkin and honey may have been eaten).

Literature Selections

The Thanksgiving Story by Alice Dalgliesh: Aladdin, 1985. (Picture book, 30 pg.) Follow a pilgrim family as they learn how to live in America and share a day of thanks with their Native neighbors.

The First Thanksgiving Feast by Joan Anderson: Clarion Books, 1984. (Informational book, 48 pg.) Pictures taken at the Plimoth (sic) Plantation Living History Museum and fictional dialogue recreate the first celebration of Thanksgiving by the Pilgrims in Plymouth, Massachusetts.

First Thanksgiving by Jean Craighead George: Philomel Books, 1993. (Picture book, 32 pg.) The story of how Pilgrims came to live and survive in New England with the help of their Native American friend, Squanto. Rich, full-page oil paintings accompany each page of text.

© Carson-Dellosa CD-2092

Squanto

Squanto was a Patuxet Indian who spoke English well because he had been to England several times before he met the Pilgrims. He was taken to England by Charles Robbins to teach the English about his people and his land. Squanto returned to America, but before he could get to his village, he was captured by fishermen and brought to Spain to be sold into slavery. He escaped to England where he boarded a ship bound for America. When he finally returned home, he found that everyone from his village had been killed by disease. This is how he came to live with the Wampanoag and eventually meet and help the Pilgrims. Squanto stayed with the Pilgrims in 1621, teaching them how to fish and catch eels and how to tell what plants were safe to eat. He also taught them to place a dead fish in the ground with corn seeds to fertilize the plants. The Pilgrims would not have had cause to celebrate the First Thanksgiving without Squanto's help. Devote a week to honoring Squanto by letting each student teach the class something he knows how to do, like Squanto did for the Pilgrims. Lessons could include how to draw a cartoon character, how to play a game, etc. Let a few students teach their lessons each day.

Promise of Friendship

In March of 1621, John Carver, Plymouth's governor, and Massasoit, the Wampanoag chief, made a peace treaty. Both parties agreed they would not hurt each others' people, they would replace or pay for any supplies taken from one another, they would help each other in case of attack by another group, and they would come unarmed on visits to each others' villages. The treaty lasted for almost 50 years because it was fair to both sides. Have students write friendship treaties with each other. Let pairs of students decide on the terms of the treaty, such as *We will take care of and return what we borrow from one another* and *We will always help each other.* Students should sign and date their treaties. Compile the treaties into a class friendship book. Students can refer to their treaties when they are not getting along to remind them of what they promised each other.

Friendship Treaty

We will take care of what we borrow and we will return it.

We will always help each other.

We will be nice to each other.

We will share crayons.

81

Corn Bread Biscuits

The Pilgrims used the corn that Squanto taught them to plant to make small cornmeal cakes. These cornmeal cakes were a substitute for the wheat cakes they ate in England. Make these corn bread biscuits, similar to the cornmeal cakes eaten at the First Thanksgiving in Plymouth.

1 cup cornmeal
4 cups water
1½ cups whole wheat flour
1 teaspoon salt

Preheat oven to 375°. Bring water and cornmeal to a boil. Reduce heat and simmer for ½ hour, stirring occasionally. Mix flour and salt thoroughly into the cornmeal. Drop biscuits (approximately ½ cup of dough each) onto an ungreased cookie sheet and press down lightly. Bake for 15 minutes, turn biscuits over and bake for 10 more minutes. Yields about 20 biscuits.

Give Thanks

Set the table for giving thanks with this 3-dimensional craft. The Pilgrims declared a day of Thanksgiving to thank God for the bountiful harvest and for Squanto, who taught them to survive in America. Had the crops not been successful, the Pilgrims would probably not have survived another year at Plymouth. Ask students to think of one or two things for which to give thanks. Instead of listing material things, like games or bikes, have them concentrate on things they need to survive, such as family members, food, etc. Have students write sentences on paper plates about the things for which they are thankful. Let each student decorate the edge of the plate with a colorful pattern and glue to the center of a 12" x 18" piece of construction paper (the placemat.) Glue a real paper napkin to the left of the plate. Then, glue on a plastic fork and spoon on either side as a place setting. Across the top of the paper write, *Setting a Table for Giving Thanks.*

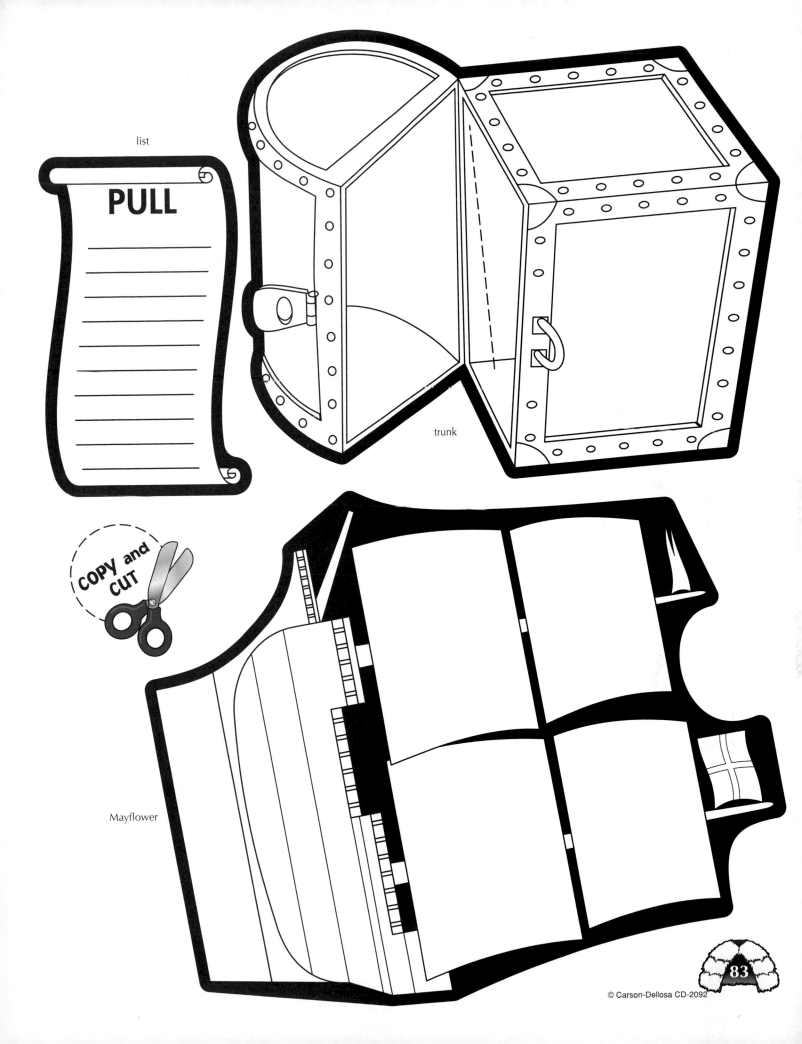

list

PULL

trunk

COPY and CUT

Mayflower

83

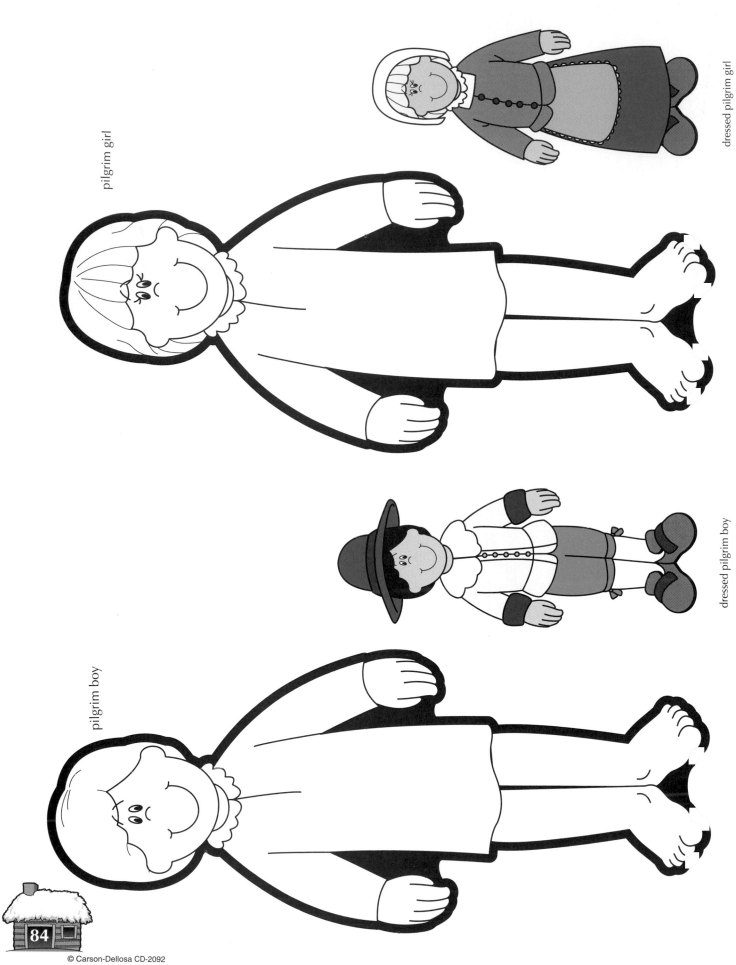

pilgrim girl

dressed pilgrim girl

pilgrim boy

dressed pilgrim boy

84

Snuggle Up With QUILTS

Learning about quilts provides real-life lessons in math and history, and helps students appreciate this traditional craft that has brought generations together.

Did You Know?

- A quilt is made by "piecing" (sewing together) scraps of fabric to make a quilt top, then "quilting" (sewing through layers) the quilt top to a layer of batting (cotton padding) and another layer of fabric.
- Quilting dates back to ancient Egypt and China when people made quilted robes to keep warm.
- When Europeans came to America, times were hard and fabric was rare and precious. Patchwork quilting became a common way to recycle old clothes and other cloth.
- During the depression, women often bought certain brands of flour that offered quality fabric sacks with pretty patterns. The women used the sacks to make patches for quilts and clothing.

Literature Selections

The Keeping Quilt by Patricia Polacco: Simon & Schuster, Inc., 1988. (Picture book, 32 pg.) Follow the life of a family quilt as it is loved and used generation after generation.

The Josefina Story Quilt by Eleanor Coerr: Harper & Row Publishers, 1986 (Chapter book, 64 pg.) A girl stitches a story quilt of her adventures on a wagon trip to California.

Sweet Clara and the Freedom Quilt by Deborah Hopkinson: Alfred A. Knopf, Inc., 1993. (Illustrated storybook, 32 pg.) A young African-American slave girl stitches a map on a quilt that shows the way to freedom.

Eight Hands Round: A Patchwork Alphabet by Ann Whitford Paul: HarperTrophy, 1996. (Picture book, 32 pg.) An alphabet of quilting patterns.

Quilt Templates

Quilters often create templates to ensure that the shapes in their quilts are the correct size. Let students use their measuring skills to make a square and a diamond template. Use a ruler to measure, draw, and cut out a 2" x 2" square and a 3 1/2" long diamond from poster board. To accurately draw the diamond, draw a 3 1/2" line, and mark a dot at 1 3/4". Then, position the ruler perpendicular to the line so that the dot matches up with the 1" mark on the ruler, and draw a 2" line. Connect the ends of each line to form the diamond. Use these templates with the activities *Friends' Autograph Quilt* (page 87), *Optical Illusion Quilt* (page 88), and *Quilting Bees* (page 89).

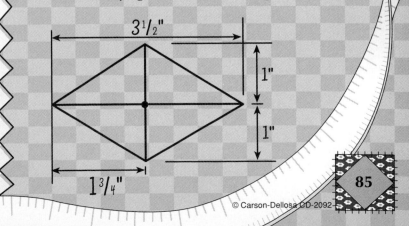

Story Quilt

Story quilts tell a story with pictures made from cloth and are usually made with a technique called *appliqué*, where fabric shapes are sewn onto a fabric background. Traditionally, story quilts told family histories, Bible stories, or documented significant life events, such as moving west. Have each student recall a personal story and turn it into a story quilt.

1. Break the story into four main parts. Create a picture of each part by gluing cut paper shapes onto a 4" x 4" white paper square.

2. Glue each picture to the center of a 5" x 5" colored paper square. (Each square should be the same color.)

3. Have students attach their squares with rubber cement, overlapping the colored borders of the squares.

4. Thread large blunt embroidery needles with yarn and let students sew running stitches around and in between their squares. "Tie" off the ends by taping them to the back of the paper. Sewing is made easier if an adult uses a push pin to punch holes along the border where the student should stitch.

5. Sew all students' finished story squares together at the corners and centers of each side, creating a class story quilt.

Sampler Quilts

Quilters often show off their stitching skills by making sampler quilts that include one of each block pattern they know how to make. To make the different blocks blend together, the same colors are used throughout. Give each student a *Quilt Blocks* worksheet (page 91, basic or page 92, advanced), and let her pick two or three colors, assign each color a number, and create a key at the top of the worksheet. Color in the quilt blocks by number. Cut out the blocks and glue them, evenly spaced apart, on a sheet of construction paper in a coordinating color. Use a pen or fine tipped marker to add stitching details around each block and to add a border pattern.

Friends' Autograph Quilt

Help students create a class autograph quilt in the spirit of friendship and cooperation. In the 1800s, autograph books and quilting were both popular, and as a result, autograph quilts were created. Autograph quilts were signed by friends and family, often with special messages. Many people were moving west in the 1800s, and autograph quilts were a comforting reminder of home. One type of autograph quilt was a friendship quilt. Pair students to create Friendship Star blocks. **1.** Let student pairs choose two colors for their square, and use their square templates (from *Quilt Templates*, page 85) to cut four triangles and four squares from one color and four triangles and one square from the other color. (Correctly sized triangles can be made by cutting a square in half diagonally.) **2.** Tape the pieces together to form a friendship star quilt block, and let each partner sign the block and write a special message of friendship if desired. **3.** Arrange the blocks together on butcher paper or a bulletin board to create your class quilt.

Crazy Quilt

Crazy quilts became popular during the Victorian period. They were made by sewing together randomly shaped pieces of fine fabrics (silk, velvet, etc.) and embroidering fancy stitches along the seams. Make beautiful crazy quilt squares from wrapping paper, wall paper samples, foil, or other interesting paper. Glue different shapes together on a square of construction paper (overlapping is okay). Trim excess paper from the edges of the square. Display a chart of several embroidery stitches commonly found on crazy quilts. Let students refer to the patterns to "embroider" over the seams in their crazy quilt square with colored glue, glitter glue, or puffy paint. Display the squares alone, or together as a class quilt.

Embroidery Stitches

Chain | Fan | Spider Web | Blanket

Feather | Zig Zag | Herringbone

87

Optical Illusion Quilt

Certain shapes and shades of colors are used to create 3-dimensional effects in quilt patterns. One popular illusion quilt is the Tumbling Blocks pattern. Talk about shades of color with students and let them each pick a color and gather three shades of paper in that color (for example, pale green, light green, dark green). If three shades are not available, use white or black for the light or dark shades (for example, white, pink, red). Use the diamond template (from *Quilt Templates*, page 85) and cut out six diamonds in each shade. Refer to the illustration (at left) to explain how to fit the diamonds together to form the tumbling blocks. Glue the diamonds to black paper for display (or to white paper if using black diamonds). Have students rotate their papers to observe the perspective.

Quilt Fractions

Use quilt squares to add a colorful twist to the study of fractions. Review basic fractions, then give each student four laminated quilt squares, each divided differently. Call out several fractions and let students fill in each section with an overhead pen, erasable marker, or grease pencil. Squares can be held up for instant checking before they are erased. Challenge older students to use blocks from the *Quilt Blocks* worksheets (pages 91-92) for the problems.

Quilt Symmetry

Students can explore symmetry by examining quilt blocks to determine which are symmetrical. A symmetrical figure can be divided in half so that each side is a mirror image of the other. Show students examples of symmetrical shapes, such as diamonds, hearts, and squares. Show how the diamond is symmetrical in two directions, the heart in one direction, and the square in three directions. Use a paper correction fluid to cover the numbers on the *Basic Quilt Blocks* worksheet (page 91), enlarge the blocks to 150%, copy onto tracing paper, and cut them out. Let students fold the patterns in half three ways (vertically, horizontally, and diagonally) and hold them up to light to see if the lines on both sides of the fold match up. If the lines match, the block is symmetrical along that fold.

Name A Quilt

Many quilt blocks have interesting names that came from everyday life. Blocks were named for trades (Anvil, Churn Dash), nature (Streak of Lightning, Bear Paw), moving to the frontier (Log Cabin, Arkansas Cross Roads), games and square dancing (Puss in the Corner, Swing in the Center), to name a few. Ask students to pick something from their lives, such as a swing set or teddy bear, then create a quilt block that resembles that item by gluing basic shapes (squares, triangles, etc.) to a square of paper. Label the finished block with its name. Combine the papers into a class quilt pattern book.

Soccer Ball

Quilting Bees

Quilting a bed-sized quilt is a big job and a quilter would often invite friends over for a quilting bee to help finish the quilt. Before telephones, the quilting bee was a perfect time to catch up on events and chat with friends. Divide students into small groups (quilting bees). Each group can make a star quilt from paper. Give each group a square yard of butcher paper and a variety of colorful construction paper. Have groups use their diamond templates (*Quilt Templates*, page 85) to cut the following number of diamonds, each number from a different color of paper: 6, 12, 18, 24, 18, 12, 6. Show students a star pattern as in the illustration (at left) and let them work together in their quilting bees to glue the diamonds into a star pattern on the butcher paper. Encourage students to chat and be social while working.

Pinwheel Patterns

Quilters use patterning skills to design new block patterns which are often variations of traditional patterns. Give each student four "patches" (four paper squares made from two colors of triangles). Model how to arrange the patches to form the Pinwheel block (at right). Show students how the patches can be turned around to make different patterns, such as Cotton Reel or Streak of Lightning (at right). Give students large ruled graph paper to record the different patterns. Encourage students to manipulate the patches to form different patterns with these four patches (they do not have to be symmetrical). After they have recorded several variations, let students choose a favorite pattern and glue the blocks to another piece of paper in that pattern.

Streak of Lightning

Pinwheel

Cotton Reel

89

Puzzling Quilts

Students can create their own quilt block puzzles to share and solve. Copy two *Basic Quilt Blocks* worksheets (page 91) for each student. Have children color both worksheets alike. Then, cut one into individual sections. (For example, cut Shoefly into nine squares, Birds in the Air into four squares, etc.) Put the pieces in a resealable plastic bag and let students exchange with each other. Have students match the square pieces on top of the complete worksheet.

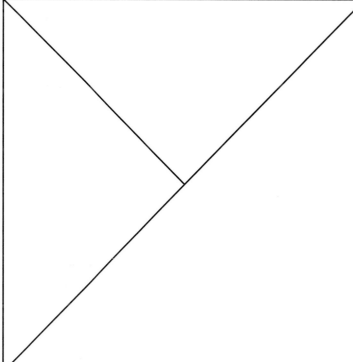

↓Pattern➡ Positions↑

Use individually-made patterns to provide patterning practice for the class! Make 32 copies of the Southern Belle patch (at left). Have students color half the patches alike with the same three colors and the remaining half alike with three different colors. Start a pattern on a bulletin board. Place the remaining patches in an envelope and let students continue the pattern.

Southern Belle patch

Basic Quilt Blocks

1 = [ ]   2 = [ ]

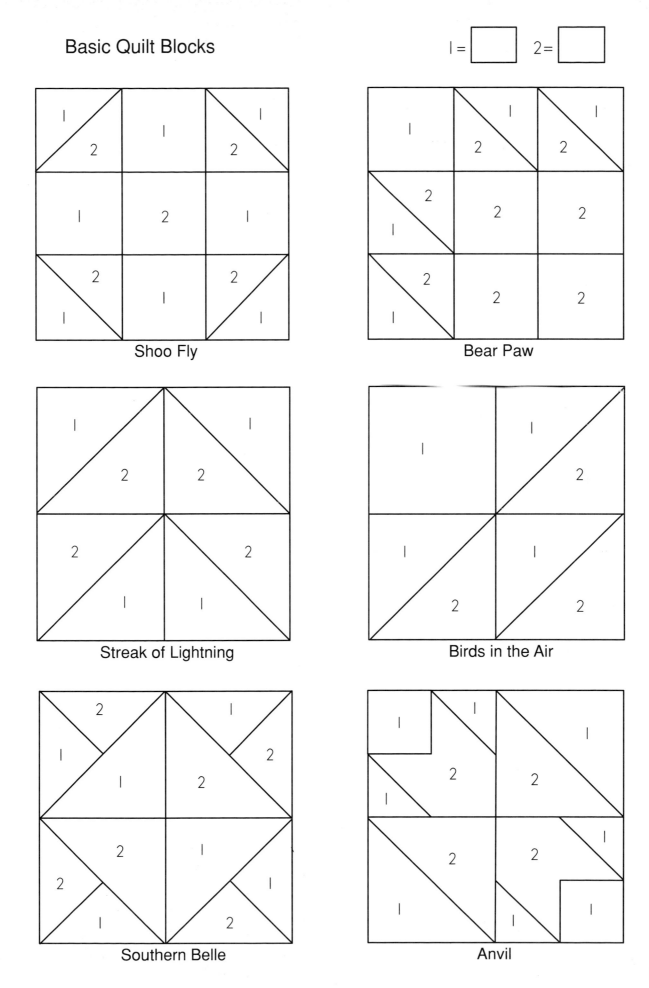

Shoo Fly

Bear Paw

Streak of Lightning

Birds in the Air

Southern Belle

Anvil

Advanced Quilt Blocks

1 = ☐ 2 = ☐ 3 = ☐

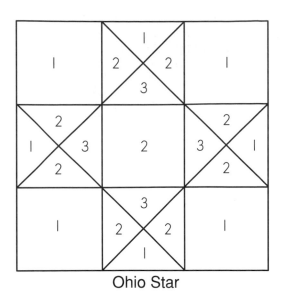

Ohio Star

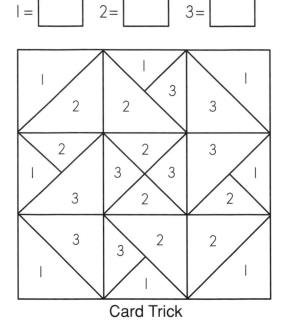

Card Trick

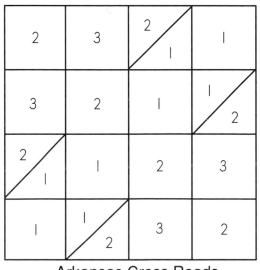

Puss in the Corner

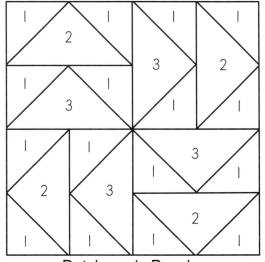

Dutchman's Puzzle

Arkansas Cross Roads

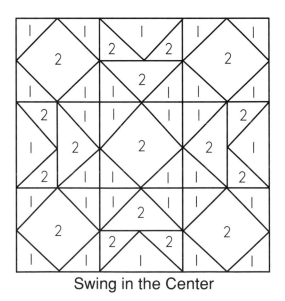

Swing in the Center

INTERNATIONAL Holidays

Day of the Dead (El Dia de Los Muertos)

This festival is held annually in Mexico on November 1 and 2. It is believed that the souls of the dead can return to the land of the living on this night. Families decorate altars with food, drink, sugar skulls, candy, flowers, and candles in their homes and in cemeteries to honor the dead and entice them to "visit" on the Day of the Dead. This is a festive occasion, not a somber one, that children and adults enjoy.

Sugary Enchiladas

Students will definitely be sweet on these yummy Mexican snacks! One traditional Mexican food is the *enchilada*—thin pancakes filled with meat. During the Day of the Dead celebration, however, Mexicans make sugar replicas of favorite foods including enchiladas. Provide butter, sugar, and cinnamon and enough tortillas for everyone in the class. Brush the tortillas with butter. Have students sprinkle the tortillas with sugar and cinnamon, then roll up the enchiladas and enjoy as a snack!

Fun in Bloom

You will know where students' smiles are "stemming" from when they make these paper flowers! The official flower for the Day of the Dead festival is the marigold. Make paper marigolds to celebrate! For each student, provide a pipe cleaner and six yellow or gold tissue paper circles cut into different sizes. Have students stack the tissue paper circles, placing the smallest one on top. Punch two holes in the center of the tissue paper circles. Have students bend the pipe cleaners in half and insert each end in one of the punched holes. Then, have students twist the ends of the pipe cleaners together to make the stems. Last, ask students to arrange the tissue paper petals any way they like. If desired, make a class paper flower arrangement to display during the days of the festival, or provide students with to/from cards to attach to the flowers and suggest that students give them to friends or relatives.

Cotton Swab Skeletons

Students will love these cotton swab skeletons! Provide each student with a plastic spoon, a piece of black construction paper, and eight cotton swabs. Have each student glue the spoon, to the construction paper. Cut four cotton swabs in half and glue the halves to each side of the spoon to represent ribs. Use whole cotton swabs as arms and legs. Have students use permanent black markers to draw eyes, noses, and teeth on the spoons. Display the skeletons on a bulletin board or wall.

93

Sint Maarten (Saint Martin's Day)

Every November 11, many people in The Netherlands celebrate *Sint Maarten*. Legend has it that Saint Martin was a soldier in the Roman army. Once when he was riding his horse, he encountered a beggar who asked him for a penny. It was bitterly cold, so Saint Martin took off his cape, ripped it into two pieces with his sword, and gave half to the beggar. He decided then that he wanted to dedicate his life to helping people and went on to become a bishop. On this night, children walk the streets carrying lanterns. They go door to door singing songs to people who give them candy, fruit, or money, much like trick-or-treating in the United States.

A Song for Saint Martin

When children go door to door collecting candy for St. Martin's Day, they must sing a song to get treats. Teach students a St. Martin's Day song to celebrate!

Saint Martin
(sing to the tune of *My Bonnie Lies Over the Ocean*)

Saint Martin once saw a poor beggar
Who needed some food and some
    clothes.
So he ripped his cape in two
    pieces
And eased some of that beggar's
    woes.

Martin, Martin
He always helped those in need,
    in need.
Martin, Martin
He was a saint, yes indeed!

Luminous Lanterns

Students will light up with joy when they make Sint Maarten lanterns! Give each student a piece of construction paper and an empty oatmeal container with a 2" hole cut into the bottom. Have students punch holes into the containers with push-pins. Supply colored pencils, crayons, glitter glue, etc., and have students draw a mural of St. Martin on the construction paper. The mural could include St. Martin meeting the beggar, dividing his cape into two pieces, helping others, etc. Next, have students wrap the murals around the oatmeal containers and tape the ends. Punch two holes in the top of the container. Give students 8" lengths of yarn for the lantern handles and instruct them to thread the yarn through the holes and tie the ends. Glue the tops to the boxes. Supply the class with a few flash-lights. Once the lanterns are made, turn off the lights. Have student shine the flashlights through the holes in the bottom of their lanterns to see them really shine!

Diwali

Diwali, also called The Festival of Lights, is celebrated by many Hindus all over the world. It occurs in either October or November. Although there are various beliefs as to how the holiday came about, the significance of the festival is consistent—it marks the triumph of brightness over darkness, good over evil, and wisdom over ignorance. Some Hindus prepare their homes days in advance. They scrub the walls and floors and make traditional sweets and cakes, such as *patashe* (a small sugar disk), which are shared with friends and neighbors. On the morning of Diwali, it is customary to take a bath in perfumed oil, don new clothes, and visit the temple. In the evening, many houses are lit up with clay lamps (called *diyas*), candles, or electric bulbs. Sparklers, firecrackers, and firework displays are enjoyed by all.

Enticing Rice Treats

Get your classroom "puffed" up with excitement by making these Diwali rice treats! During Diwali, Indians buy puffed rice by the kilogram. One kilogram is over 2 pounds of puffed rice! The rice is offered to Lakshmi, the goddess of prosperity, in the hopes that she will come and bless their homes. All participants in the festival want Lakshmi to come to their homes since Diwali marks the beginning of the Hindu new year. Friends and family also receive puffed rice during the festival. Provide students with 9" x 9" squares of different colored plastic wrap. Give each student about one cup of puffed rice cereal for each treat. Have students place the puffed rice cereal in the middle of the plastic wrap squares. Next, ask students to twist the plastic wrap around the puffed rice. Supply students with 12" pieces of ribbon or string. Tell students to tie the ribbons around the tops of the rice treats to seal the bag. Encourage students to give the treats to close friends or family members.

Decorative Diwali Designs

"Flooring" students with enthusiasm will be easy when you let them make these traditional Diwali decorations! To get ready for Diwali, Hindus make *rangoli* on the floors of their homes. Rangoli are colorful designs made from rice flour that are meant to welcome visitors during the holiday. Provide students with dark construction paper and a variety of colorful chalk. Allow students to design their rangoli any way they choose. Once the designs are completed, coat them with a spray fixative. When the designs are dry, display them on a bulletin board.

Diwali (continued)

Paper Oil Lamps

Brighten your classroom by having students create their own lamp designs to represent the lights that shine during Diwali. Provide children with a pieces of construction paper to fold vertically. Instruct students to draw half of a lamp design extending away from the center fold. Cut out the lamp half, unfold it, and glue the design to paper. Add gold glitter flames for extra sparkle.

Holiday Clothes

Since it is customary to wear new clothes on Diwali, have students design special new outfits for themselves! Give each student a piece of construction paper on which to draw a self-portrait. Provide wallpaper and fabric scraps and have students cut clothing shapes to glue to their self-portraits. Have students share their new holiday outfits with the class. Display the completed projects on a bulletin board.

Shiny Sparklers

Give each student a straw, four pipe cleaners, orange construction paper, glue, and gold glitter. Cut burst shapes from the construction paper and add glitter. Glue to the ends of the pipe cleaners. Then, let each student stick the pipe cleaners into the opening of the straw. Display the sparklers on a table or window sill.

GLUE

Gold Glitter